CIVIL AND POLITICAL RIGHTS IN CROATIA

G000155197

Human Rights Watch/Helsinki

Human Rights Watch
New York ● Washington ● Los Angeles ● London ● Brussels

Library of Congress Catalog Card Number: 95-75413
ISBN 1-56432-148-7

Human Rights Watch/Helsinki
Human Rights Watch/Helsinki was established in 1978 to monitor and promote domestic and international compliance with the human rights provisions of the 1975 Helsinki Accords. It is affiliated with the International Helsinki Federation for Human Rights, which is based in Vienna, Austria. Holly Cartner is the executive director; Erika Dailey, Rachel Denber, Ivana Nizich and Christopher Panico are research associates; Ivan Lupis is the research assistant; Anne Kuper, Alexander Petrov and Lenee Simon are associates. Jonathan Fanton is the chair of the advisory committee and Alice Henkin is vice chair.

HUMAN RIGHTS WATCH

ACKNOWLEDGMENTS

This report is based on long-term research conducted by Željka Markić, consultant to Human Rights Watch/Helsinki, and Ivana Nizich, Research Associate of Human Rights Watch/Helsinki, between February 1992 and December 1994. This report was written by Ivana Nizich, and was edited by Jeri Laber, Senior Advisor to Human Rights Watch. Anne Kuper provided production assistance.

Human Rights Watch/Helsinki expresses its appreciation to organizations, groups and individuals active in Croatia's human rights movement, to other non-governmental and refugee organizations, and to members of Croatia's political and ethnic and national communities for their assistance with this report. Human Rights Watch/Helsinki also acknowledges the cooperation of the Croatian government with requests related to information contained in segments of this report.

CONTENTS

I. INTRODUCTION

The Croatian government has taken steps to correct some of the abuses of human rights that had marked Croatia's first two years of independence, but violations of civil and political rights by reason of ethnic identity and political dissent continue.[1] On February 13, 1992, Human Rights Watch/Helsinki (formerly Helsinki Watch) sent a letter to Croatian President Franjo Tudjman delineating violations of human rights and humanitarian law in Croatia during 1990 and 1991.[2] This report describes the status of civil and political rights in Croatia since then. This report does not address violations of the rules of war perpetrated by Croatian and Serbian armed forces in Croatia nor does it address the situation of human rights in Serbian-controlled areas of Croatia. Both subjects have been addressed in previous Human Rights Watch/Helsinki reports and will be addressed in forthcoming reports. Furthermore, this report does not deal with violations by Croatian or Bosnian Croat forces in Bosnia-Hercegovina, which Human Rights Watch/Helsinki has documented and will continue to report.[3] However, this report addresses the treatment of Bosnian refugees living in Croatia.

Although the behavior of the police force improved, and physical attacks against Serbs and their property had declined from late 1992 to 1994, police abuse and attacks against Serbs and their property have increased in 1995, primarily in relation to recent military offensives that re-captured the formerly Serb-controlled areas of western Slavonia and Krajina.[4] The government continues to impede

---

[1] This report provides an overview of events that occurred in 1992, 1993, and, to a lesser extent, in 1994 and 1995.

[2] Helsinki Watch, Letter to Franjo Tudjman, President of the Republic of Croatia, February 13, 1992. The Croatian government's response to the letter is attached to this report as appendix A.

[3] For accounts of abuses by Croatian and Bosnian Croat forces in Bosnia-Hercegovina, see the following Human Rights Watch/Helsinki reports: *War Crimes in Bosnia-Hercegovina, Volume I*, August 1992, *War Crimes in Bosnia-Hercegovina, Volume II*, April 1993, and "Bosnia-Hercegovina: Violations of the Rules of War by Bosnian Croat and Muslim Forces in Central and Southwestern Bosnia-Hercegovina," September 1993.

[4] This report does not include violations of humanitarian and human rights law during and after the Croatian Army offensives in western Slavonia or in the so-called Krajina area, which includes the regions of Banija, Lika, Kordun, and part of the Dalmatian hinterland.

freedom of the press and expression. Although Croatia's Interior Ministry has taken steps to check abusive behavior of the police, the behavior of the military police has worsened dramatically in the past three years. Indeed, organs of the Defense Ministry are responsible for many of the human rights abuses in Croatia today. The Ministry of Defense has repeatedly refused to respect the judgments of the courts, and members of the Croatian Army and military police show increasing disdain for the rule of law and the civilian authorities. Gojko Šušak, Croatia's Defense Minister, and Mate Laušić, the chief of Croatia's military police, have not taken serious steps to correct the behavior of Croatia's military police. Although domestic human rights organizations, opposition politicians and some members of the Croatian government and ruling Croatian Democratic Union (*Hrvatska Demokratska Zajednica* - HDZ) have publicly protested against the behavior of Croatia's Defense Ministry, Croatian President Franjo Tudjman has not taken firm steps to correct abusive behavior within branches of his government.

In some instances, abuses of civil and political rights in Croatia are indirectly or directly associated with the wars in Croatia and Bosnia-Hercegovina.

●   Continued tensions between Croatian and Serbian forces in parts of Croatia, rebel Serbian control of one-third of Croatia's territory and fighting between Muslims and Croats in Bosnia in 1993[5] has been accompanied by animosity, harassment and discrimination against Serbs, Muslims and other non-Croats who are law-abiding citizens of Croatia. Refusal of citizenship, job dismissals and other forms of discrimination have socially, economically and politically marginalized thousands of non-Croats who have lived in Croatia for many years or decades. Lack of

---

For an account of abuses perpetrated during the western Slavonia offensive, see Human Rights Watch/Helsinki, "Croatia: The Croatian Army Offensive in Western Slavonia and Its Aftermath," (New York: Human Rights Watch, July 1995), which contains information available as of June 10, 1995; United Nations Economic and Social Council, "Situation of human rights in the former Yugoslavia, Periodic report submitted by Mr. Tadeusz Mazowiecki, Special Rapporteur of the Commission on Human Rights, pursuant to paragraph 42 of Commission resolution 1995/89," E/CN.4/1996/6, 5 July 1995, pp. 4-13; and United Nations Security Council, "Report of the Secretary-General Submitted Pursuant to Security Council Resolution 981 (1995)," S/1995/650, 3 August 1995.

[5] Full-scale war broke out between Bosnian Croat and the predominantly Muslim forces of the Bosnian government in 1993; since then, the two have reconciled and a federation between the two groups has been formed in parts of Bosnia-Hercegovina that are not controlled by rebel Serbian forces.

free broadcast media sources and harassment of the independent press has served to perpetuate inter-ethnic tensions.

- Some Serbs, former Yugoslav Army (*Jugoslavenska Narodna Armija* - JNA) personnel and others continue to be forcibly evicted from their respective homes, usually without respect to the persons' right to due process and often with the acquiescence of the local authorities and Croatia's Ministry of Defense.

- The influx of Bosnian Croat refugees from central Bosnia who were displaced by Bosnian government and Muslim forces in 1993 was followed by the worsening treatment of Bosnian Muslim refugees living in Croatia at that time.

- The prolonged war has resulted in lax discipline among Croatian Army troops and the military police, who are largely responsible for most abuses perpetrated against persons in detention. There is little evidence of efforts to check abuses by these military forces.

In other instances, violations of civil and political rights are associated with Croatia's communist past and its status as a republic of the former Socialist Federal Republic of Yugoslavia (Socijalistička Federativna Republika Jugoslavia - SFRJ). Claiming that Croatia is in transition from a socialist to a capitalist economy, the Croatian government has sometimes used this as justification for deliberately hampering the development of a genuinely free press in Croatia through a variety of mechanisms. The granting of citizenship has been denied arbitrarily to some non-Croats, despite the fact that these persons have lived in Croatia for decades. The ownership of property which formerly had belonged to Yugoslavia's communist party, the Yugoslav Army or other federal organs of the former SFRJ was transferred to the Croatian government, which then arbitrarily forced the eviction from their state-owned homes of persons formerly affiliated with organs of the previous regime.

To its credit, the Croatian government continues to cooperate with international and to a lesser extent, domestic human rights groups and delegations concerned about human rights in Croatia. In March 1993, Tadeusz Mazowiecki, the Special Rapporteur for the Former Yugoslavia of the United Nations Commission on Human Rights, established a field office in Zagreb. Local and national government officials — including high-ranking members of the Croatian government — frequently meet with human rights activists to discuss their grievances. International and domestic human rights groups are generally allowed to function without direct government interference in Croatia.

II. CITIZENSHIP

GENERAL PRINCIPLES AND INTERNATIONAL LAW

Citizenship determines the enjoyment of certain fundamental civil and political rights, as well as being a precondition for the receipt of welfare benefits and other government entitlements on which many depend for their livelihood. International law gives states great — though not unlimited — freedom in setting requirements for citizenship. According to article 1 of the 1930 Hague Convention on Certain Questions Relating to the Conflict of Nationality Laws:

> it is for each state to determine under its own law who are citizens ... [but] the citizenship law of a State shall be recognized by other states only insofar as it is consistent with international conventions, international customs and the principles of law generally recognized with regard to citizenship.[6]

Following the precedent of the 1930 Hague Convention on Nationality, article 1(3) of the 1965 International Convention on the Elimination of All Forms of Racial Discrimination (CERD) states that:

> Nothing in this Convention may be interpreted as affecting in any way the legal provisions of State parties concerning nationality, citizenship or naturalization, provided that such provisions do not discriminate against any particular community.[7]

Max van der Stoel, the High Commissioner on National Minorities of the Organization on Security and Cooperation in Europe (OSCE), has recommended that, "in view of articles 1(3) and 5(d) of the CERD, any discrimination on the ground of nationality or ethnicity should be avoided when enacting or

---

[6]Kees Groenendijk, "Nationality, Minorities and Statelessness: The Case of the Baltic States," *Helsinki Monitor* (Netherlands Helsinki Committee), Vol. 4, Issue 3, 1993. See also Human Rights Watch/Helsinki, "Integrating Estonia's Non-Citizen Minority," (New York: Human Rights Watch, October 1993), pp. 11-12.

[7] *Twenty-Four Human Rights Documents*, (New York: Center for the Study of Human Rights, Columbia University, 1992).

implementing legal provisions concerning nationality, citizenship or naturalization."[8]

The Council of Europe has also stated that "citizenship should not be granted arbitrarily and in violation of the principle of non-discrimination, a rule found in most human rights treaties."[9] The Council recognized that article 15(1) of the Universal Declaration of Human Rights grants everyone the right to citizenship and states that no one shall be arbitrarily deprived of his or her citizenship.[10] The Council also points out that children have the right to acquire citizenship under article 24(3) of the U.N. Covenant on Civil and Political Rights and article 7(1) of the Convention on the Rights of the Child.[11] All of these legal principles are aimed at avoiding statelessness among the world's population, a condition which the 1954 Convention Relating to the Status of Stateless Persons and the 1961 Convention on the Reduction of Statelessness seek to abolish.[12]

Despite the general principles set forth by the international community and regional European bodies, international law does not address the issue of citizenship in detail. For this reason, Human Rights Watch/Helsinki has adopted a position identifying principles that we believe should be embodied in new citizenship laws and proposals.[13] We believe that the newly formed states that have emerged from the former Socialist Federal Republic of Yugoslavia (SFRJ) have an obligation to adopt and apply citizenship laws that treat in a fair and non-discriminatory manner individuals who moved to or otherwise lived in the

---

[8] Letter from Max van der Stoel, the Organization on Security and Cooperation in Europe (OSCE) High Commissioner on National Minorities, to Trivimi Velliste, Foreign Minister of the Republic of Estonia, April 6, 1993.

[9] Council of Europe, "Comments on the Draft Citizenship Law of the Republic of Latvia," Strasbourg, January 24, 1994.

[10] *Ibid.*

[11] *Ibid.*

[12] Croatia is a party to both Conventions.

[13] Human Rights Watch/Helsinki's position on citizenship in the republics of the former SFRJ is contained in Appendix C of this report. See also Helsinki Watch, "New Citizenship Laws in the Republics of the Former USSR," (New York: Human Rights Watch, April 15, 1992).

respective republics of the SFRJ when it was a unified state.[14] Unfortunately, citizenship laws and proposals in some of the republics of the former SFRJ — including Croatia — have been applied in ways that discriminate against ethnic and national groups which are not the majority group in the respective republic.

It should be noted, however, that following domestic and international crticism, the Croatian government sometimes reversed earlier denials of citizenship to non-Croats who were long-term residents of Croatia. In general, reports concerning the denial of citizenship based solely on the applicant's ethnicity declined in 1994, but denial of citizenship to Serbs who remained in formerly Serb-held areas of western Slavonia and Krajina in mid-1995 have recently been reported and may be a problem in the future.

CRITERIA FOR FAIRNESS

Citizenship laws in newly independent states should be evaluated by two dependent sets of criteria: first, whether the law refrains from treating as immigrants certain individuals who lived on the state's territory before the declaration of independence;[15] and second, if the law does treat such individuals as immigrants, by the qualifications according to which the former may accede to or be denied citizenship. Such qualifications typically include minimum residence requirements, language proficiency, and proof of legal source of income. They also sometimes include medical, political, and financial grounds upon which a group of individuals could be excluded from citizenship.

The most liberal citizenship law is the "zero option," which grants citizenship to all people living in the republic either at the time independence was declared or when the law was adopted. It generally sets out a certain period during which individuals either may apply for citizenship or automatically become citizens provided they do not officially reject citizenship in a given state.

Human Rights Watch/Helsinki views with concern various laws and proposals under consideration in states of the former SFRJ that could exclude from

---

[14] The following principles set forth in this section also were applied by Human Rights Watch/Helsinki with regard to citizenship laws in the now independent republics of the former Soviet Union. See Helsinki Watch, "New Citizenship Laws in the Republics of the Former USSR," (New York: Human Rights Watch, April 15, 1992).

[15] That is, whether it sets out for these people citizenship regulations that are separate from those that apply to other individuals currently seeking to move to the new state.

citizenship in the state in question many individuals with significant links to that state. Those excluded are individuals who, while the SFRJ was a unified state, took up residence in a former Yugoslav republic that did not coincide with his or her ethno-national identity and now find themselves resident in a new state in which their ethnicity/nationality is not the dominant one. We believe that most individuals who migrated from one republic to another could not have foreseen the change in the SFRJ's political status and that they lived in any given republic with the expectation that their residence would not be interrupted by the issue of their citizenship.

Human Rights Watch/Helsinki believes that the denial of citizenship to persons who have extensive social and cultural ties to the community but who are members of the minority population in each of the respective republics of the former SFRJ is discriminatory against the minority group in question. It also leads to the social and economic marginalization of the minority population, forcing people to leave one republic and emigrate to a republic in which they would be part of the majority but which they do not otherwise consider their home.

Denial of Croatian citizenship to some Serbs, Muslims and members of other ethnic groups renders them illegal aliens in their own country. Denying citizenship to deserving individuals would violate their voting rights guaranteed in Article 25 of the International Covenant on Civil and Political Rights (ICCPR). Moreover, the allocation of property and other social and economic rights often hinges upon citizenship. Citizenship laws that exclude otherwise deserving individuals would create categories of people whose civil and political rights would be routinely violated and whose eligibility for medical, welfare, educational and other benefits would be denied.

Some Serbs who fled from western Slavonia and Krajina during or after the Croatian Army offensives in these areas in May and August 1995 may at some point in the future want to return to Croatia. The Croatian government should not unnecessarily hamper these Serbs' applications for Croatian citizenship, if they choose to apply for such status and return to their homes in Croatia in the future.

CROATIA'S LAW ON CITIZENSHIP AND ITS APPLICATION

After Croatia seceded from the SFRJ in 1991, all residents in Croatia were required to apply for a "*domovnica*," which certifies a person's Croatian citizenship. The Ministry of Interior is responsible for granting citizenship, which is regulated by the Law on Croatian Citizenship.[16] The law specifies the conditions a person must meet before he or she is granted citizenship. Although the "zero option" generally has been applied to ethnic Croats from Croatia, non-Croats — and to a lesser extent, Croats from other former SFRJ republics — must meet more stringent criteria if they are to receive citizenship. The Croatian citizenship law does not adequately take into account the fact that Croatia was once part of the SFRJ and that many of Croatia's long-time residents do not qualify for citizenship under the new law because they are neither Croats by ethnicity nor were they born in Croatia.[17]

The granting of citizenship in Croatia has been marred by long delays, ethnic discrimination, arbitrary decisions and a lack of fair and consistent procedure founded in law. Since mid-1992, the government's administrative organs have taken steps to reverse decisions that arbitrarily denied many people Croatian citizenship.

Non-Croats who have lived in Croatia for decades do not automatically receive citizenship. A child of Croatian parents who was born and raised in Canada and has never visited Croatia can more easily obtain Croatian citizenship than can a Serb, Muslim or Albanian who was born in a one of the other republics of the former SFRJ but has lived in Croatia for decades. The denial of citizenship to long-term residents of Croatia who are not of Croatian nationality arbitrarily strips such persons of rights they had previously enjoyed. The former Special Rapporteur for the U.N. Commission on Human Rights for the former Yugoslavia[18] has rightly pointed out the following:

---

[16] "Zakon o hrvatskom državljanstvu," *Narodne Novine*, No. 53/91. The citizenship law was amended on May 8, 1992, and references made to the law in this report are cited from the amended version. (Amendments to the citizenship law are contained in *Narodne Novine*, No. 28/92.)

[17] Article 3 of the Law on Croatian Citizenship states:
Croatian citizenship is acquired by:
1. one's origin
2. birth on the territory of the Republic of Croatia
3. naturalization
4. by international agreements.

[18] Hereinafter referred to as U.N. Special Rapporteur. Tadeusz Mazowiecki resigned as the U.N. Special Rapporteur on July 27, 1995, protesting the international community's "slow and ineffectual" response to human rights abuses in Bosnia.

The Croatian authorities have repeatedly justified the policy of ethnic differentiation in the conferment of citizenship by comparing Croatian legislation with the legislation of other States which they say make similar distinctions on the basis of descent. It is, however, imperative to distinguish the citizenship law of a State dealing with immigration under ordinary circumstances, where the applicant may have no social attachment to the territory concerned, as opposed to a new State where denial of citizenship on the basis of ethnic or national origin affects those who have previously enjoyed citizenship of the predecessor State and lawful residence on the territory concerned.[19]

The Croatian government has defended its decision to deny some non-Croats and those not born in Croatia citizenship. The Croatian government has claimed that each of the former SFRJ republics should be allowed to decide whether or not to grant citizenship to former SFRJ citizens living in the republic in question and that this matter should be settled by bilateral agreements between the states of the former SFRJ.[20] This pre-supposes that a person denied citizenship in one republic could obtain citizenship in another republic of the former SFRJ. While this may be a valid assertion in many cases, such an approach does not take into account the residency, ownership of property and family ties of the person in question. For example, a Serb born in Serbia in the 1940s who had emigrated to and lived in Croatia since the 1950s could be denied Croatian citizenship and granted Serbian citizenship, despite the fact that all his or her personal and professional ties are in Croatia, not in Serbia.

Those persons who have been denied Croatian citizenship but otherwise have lived, worked and owned property in Croatia for most of their adult lives are now considered illegally employed and ineligible for welfare benefits and pensions, and their ownership of property is precarious. They cannot be employed in the civil

---

[19] U.N. Commission on Human Rights, "Situation of Human Rights in the Territory of the Former Yugoslavia: Fifth periodic report on the situation of human rights in the territory of the former Yugoslavia submitted by Mr. Tadeusz Mazowiecki, Special Rapporteur of the Commission on Human Rights, pursuant to paragraph 32 of Commission resolution 1993/7 of 23 February 1993," E/CN.4/1994/47, November 17, 1993, p. 17.

[20] This option also has been proposed by the Working Group on Succession at the International Conference on the Former Yugoslavia.

service and are not always entitled to the medical services or free education available to citizens. Given their precarious residency and socio-economic status, such persons — most frequently non-Croats — are forced to leave Croatia.

The Employment Law for Foreigners requires that all non-Croatian citizens obtain a work permit in order to work in Croatia. Those persons denied Croatian citizenship who are not granted work permits can be dismissed from their jobs, despite the fact that they may have been employed in a given enterprise for many years. The Croatian government has on at least four occasions extended the date by which persons were to apply for work permits or risk dismissal from their jobs. The Central Employment Agency in Zagreb decides in each case whether a person is to obtain a work permit. According to Croatian law, a work permit can only be issued to a foreigner if he or she retains specific qualifications which cannot otherwise be filled from among Croatia's citizens. The high unemployment rate among Croats who have citizenship is a factor in government decisions to grant work permits to non-Croats who do not possess Croatian citizenship.

Human Rights Watch/Helsinki interviewed scores of people — almost exclusively non-Croats — who had lived in Croatia for more than the past ten years but still were refused citizenship, often without reason. Human Rights Watch/Helsinki retains copies of more than sixty notices issued by the Ministry of Interior in Zagreb in which the applicants' requests for Croatian citizenship were denied. Most of those denied citizenship were born in one of the republics of the former SFRJ other than Croatia. Articles 8 and 26 of the Croatian citizenship law are most frequently cited as justification for the denial of citizenship.

The denial of citizenship is based on allegations that the person did not meet the requirements set forth in Article 8, clause 1, of the citizenship law which states:

> Croatian citizenship may be acquired by assimilation by a foreigner who submitted the application for Croatian citizenship and fulfills the following conditions:
>
> 1. That he [or she] has reached 18 years of age and is able to work.
>
> 2. That he [or she] is permitted to give up his [or her] foreign citizenship, or that he [or she] has proof that this permit will be given in case he [or she] is granted Croatian citizenship.

4. That he [or she] is familiar with the Croatian language and Latin alphabet.

5. That it can be assumed from his [or her] behavior that he [or she] respects the laws and customs of the Republic of Croatia and that he [or she] accepts Croatian culture.

When point 5[21] of Article 8 is cited as justification for rejection of citizenship, the rejection notice does not specifically state how an applicant's behavior reflects disrespect for the laws, customs and culture of Croatia. The clause is ambiguous and open to misuse and the application of subjective criteria to deny a person citizenship. In cases of rejection under Article 8, the rejected applicant can initiate administrative proceedings before the Administrative Court of Croatia within thirty days after receipt of the rejection notice.

Article 10 of the law allows for a foreign citizen to become a Croatian citizen if he or she is married to a Croatian citizen and has been granted permanent residency on the territory of Croatia. However, in many cases, some members of a family are granted citizenship while others are not. Human Rights Watch/Helsinki spoke to many such families in the past three years. The following scenario is typical. Jelena,[22] a Croatian woman, and Zvonimir, one of her two sons who was born in Zagreb, apply for and receive Croatian citizenship. However, Haris, her Bosnian-born Muslim husband, and Dušan, her other son who was born in Serbia, are denied citizenship despite the fact that they have spent most of their adult lives and childhoods in Croatia. In such cases, families are in danger of being separated, given the illegal status of some of their members.

Others have applied for citizenship but have not been informed of a decision for months and in some cases over one year, leaving them uncertain about their status in Croatia. In other instances, persons who have fled or originally are from rebel Serbian-controlled areas of Croatia cannot travel to these areas to obtain their birth certificates and other identity and residency documents. Without such documents, some people have been refused Croatian citizenship.

---

[21] A third article requiring the uninterrupted residence of at least five years on the territory of the Republic of Croatia was dropped from the revised citizenship law on May 8, 1992. The citation of the articles of the citizenship law, in this case, is based on the original law, prior to its May 1992 revision.

[22] The names used here are fictional.

Still others who do not have or have been denied Croatian citizenship have been expelled from the country. Z.L., a Serbian resident of Split, was issued a notice by the division of administrative affairs of the police in Split. According to the police notice, the residency of Z.L., "a citizen of Serbia," was revoked. The notice stated that Z.L. was to leave Croatia by May 5, 1993, and that he did not have the right to return until May 5, 1995.[23] The notice stated that Z.L.'s residency in Croatia was being revoked at the request of the division for operative affairs of the Split police, which cited article 42, clause 1(3) of Croatia's Law on the Movement and Residency of Foreigners as justification for the request.[24] Z.L.'s expulsion may have been a consequence of his having lodged a complaint against the military, after soldiers broke into his apartment.

Z.L. had a right to appeal the decision, which his lawyer did on April 1, 1993. According to the lawyer's appeal, Z.L. had lived in Croatia since 1964 and worked at the police station until 1987, when he retired. His deceased wife was a Croat and his two daughters were born and continue to reside in Split. All of Z.L.'s immediate relatives in Split are Croats. Despite the fact that Z.L. considers Croatia to be his home and has lived there for twenty-nine of his fifty-eight years, he was expelled from Croatia.[25]

The citizenship law does not adequately set out the procedures that the Ministry of Interior must follow in accepting or rejecting a person's application for citizenship. In many instances, the decision as to whether or not a person's application will be denied is made at the whim of the issuing administrative officer at the local police station. Particularly in cases where the person is a long-time resident of Croatia but is not a Croat by ethnicity, the denial or granting of citizenship has been arbitrarily decided. Human Rights Watch/Helsinki spoke to some individuals who, after having been denied citizenship, complained to a higher

---

[23] Republika Hrvatska, Ministarstvo Unutarnjih Poslova, Policijska Uprava Split, Odjel za Upravne Poslove, Odsjek za putovnice, strance, oružje, državljanstvo i javne skupove, Broj: 511-12-08/1, Split, March 25, 1993.

[24] Article 42, clause 1 (3) of the Law on the Movement and Residence of Foreigners states: "A person's permanent residency status shall be revoked: ... 3. if this is so required in order to protect the national security and legal order [of the state] ..." (See "Zakon o kretanju i boravku stranaca," *Narodne Novine*, 53/91.) For a further account regarding the events leading up to Z.L.'s expulsion, see the section concerning prosecution of Croatian Army soldiers and police officers.

[25] See section concerning the prosecution of Croatian Army soldiers and police officers.

official. In some cases, the superior officer overturned the decision of the administrative personnel, claiming that the administrative officer had no grounds to deny the applicant citizenship.

Croatia established at least three alien reception centers where people who received expulsion or banishment orders, whose residence permits had been revoked or who resided without the authorization of Croatia but have not been expelled are detained pursuant to the Law on the Movement and Residence of Aliens.[26] Those held in the Dugo Selo center near Zagreb did not receive a judicial or administrative decision confining them to the center for a specified period of time.[27] According to the Office for Migration in the Interior Ministry, an alien is assigned to an alien reception center in the absence of an agreement with the embassy of the country of which the alien is a citizen to transfer him or her to that country.[28] However, some of the aliens in the reception centers are not citizens of another country, but citizens of the former SFRJ who had been living in Croatia for many years with members of their family and real property, but had been denied Croatian citizenship.[29]

On May 24, 1993, Croatia's Constitutional Court examined challenges and revisions to the citizenship law proposed by a variety of opposition political parties. In its ruling, the court did not support a broad interpretation of the law which would have been more favorable to non-Croats applying for citizenship. However, it did rule that Article 26 of the citizenship law — which allowed the Ministry of Interior to deny citizenship to an applicant who otherwise met the legally prescribed requirements needed for the acquisition of citizenship — allowed the Ministry of Interior to deny citizenship without reason and that such action was unconstitutional. Article 26, which may have been intended to address exceptional cases involving national security questions, had been used to deny scores of non-Croats Croatian citizenship.

---

[26] United Nations Security Council, Annex to "Human Rights Questions: Human Rights Situations and Reports of Special Rapporteurs and Representatives," *Situation of human rights in the former Yugoslavia: Note by the Secretary General*, A/49/641,S/1994/1252, November 4, 1994, p. 27. See also *Narodne Novine*, No. 53, October 8, 1991, pp. 1482-89.

[27] *Ibid.*

[28] *Ibid.*

[29] *Ibid.*

Croatia's Constitutional Court ruled that the Interior Ministry had to define the circumstances under which the granting of citizenship to an applicant would be detrimental to the interests of Croatia by defining what it considered to be "the interests of the state." The Court pointed to Article 206(3) of Croatia's Law on General Administrative Procedure which requires that all written judgements must give a reason for the decision.

On December 8, 1993, the Constitutional Court again examined the citizenship law and struck down Article 26 altogether. The Court stated that persons denied citizenship were guaranteed the right to appeal.

Although the Constitutional Court's decision may mitigate the arbitrariness of the Interior Ministry's decision-making process, the Court did not directly address the ability of the Defense Ministry to reject an applicant's request for citizenship without reason. Article 32 of Croatia's citizenship law states that "military matters concerning Croatian citizenship are dealt with by the Minister of Defense." The law fails to define or cite examples of "military matters concerning Croatian citizenship," nor does the law specify whether a person has a right to appeal the Defense Ministry's decision if his or her application for citizenship is denied in such a case. It is unclear whether the December 1993 judgment of Croatia's Constitutional Court guaranteeing persons the right to an appeal is afforded to those denied citizenship by the Defense Ministry. Although the Defense Ministry rarely engages in citizenship questions, in the absence of court instructions similar to those issued for the Interior Ministry, the vague reference to "military matters concerning Croatian citizenship" in Article 32 leaves a loophole through which an application for citizenship can still be arbitrarily denied by the state.

III. TREATMENT OF SERBS AND OTHER MINORITIES IN CROATIA[30]

Direct attacks against Serbs and their property in Croatia generally decreased between 1992 and early 1995. This was due, in part, to the fact that fierce fighting between Serbian and Croatian forces in Croatia subsided following the establishment of a ceasefire and the nominal acceptance of the Vance plan in January 1992.[31] Attacks against Serbs also decreased during that period because many Serbs had left Croatian government-controlled areas, and those that remained were sometimes considered to be "loyal" to, or to have accepted the authority of, the Croatian government.

However, following the re-capture of the so-called Krajina region from rebel Serbian authorities in August 1995, Croatian soldiers have burned Serbian villages and destroyed property belonging to Serbs. As of mid-August 1995, these crimes apparently are being conducted with impunity and appear aimed at preventing the return of those Serbs who had lived in the area but who fled during the offensive. Following the re-capture of the western Slavonia area in May 1995, Croatian forces harassed, threatened and robbed Serbs who chose to remain in the area. Persons held in detention also were beaten or otherwise mistreated following their capture.[32] Graves containing the remains of those killed during the fighting

---

[30] This section deals primarily with the treatment of Serbs living in areas of Croatia which remained under Croatian-government control as of December 1994. As stated earlier, abuses associated with the Croatian Army's May and August 1995 offensives in western Slavonia and the Krajina region, respectively, are or will be contained in other or subsequent Human Rights Watch/Helsinki reports. The status of human rights following the offensives in these two areas will briefly be summarized in this section.

[31] Under the January 1992 ceasefire agreement, commonly known as the "Vance plan," troops of the United Nations Protection Force (UNPROFOR) were deployed in three regions of Croatia, starting in mid-May. For a description and critique of the UNPROFOR mission in the former Yugoslavia, see Human Rights Watch, *The Lost Agenda: Human Rights and U.N. Field Operations*, (New York: Human Rights Watch, June 1993), pp. 75-105.

[32] As of August 9, 1995, the International Committee of the Red Cross (ICRC) has visited and registered 353 Serbs detained by Croatian authorities following the Krajina offensive. The ICRC also visited 107 Serbs detained by Bosnian government forces near Bihać.

have yet to be exhumed by independent forensic experts and the identities of all those killed during the offensive have yet to be released by the Croatian government.

Federal election law provides for the representation of all minorities in parliament,[33] with proportional representation guaranteed for any minority that comprises more than 8 percent of the population.[34] According to the 1991 census, Serbs comprised approximately 11.5 percent of the population in Croatia and were the only non-Croatian ethnic group in Croatia that met the 8 percent criteria for parliamentary representation.[35] Thirteen of the 138 seats in House of Representatives of Croatia's parliament were allotted to members of Croatia's Serbian population.[36] The Federal Election Commission designated thirteen Serbs

---

[33] When Croatia was still part of the SFRJ, the republic's parliament consisted of three chambers:

    1. the social-political chamber (društveno političko vijeće)

    2. the chamber of municipalities (viječe opčina)

    3. the chamber of associated labor (viječe udruženog rada)

Since its secession from the SFRJ in 1991, Croatia has re-structured its parliament. Institutions associated with Tito's system of "self-management" (a Yugoslav variation of socialist economic theory) were abolished, including the Croatian parliament's socio-political chamber and the chamber of associated labor.

The chamber of municipalities was re-structured and a bicameral legislature was formed. Currently, the higher house of the Croatian parliament — formed in March 1993 — is the House of Counties (županijski dom) which represents Croatia's twenty-one counties (županije). Each county (županija) is represented in parliament by a governor/prefect (župan). The lower house of parliament is known as the House of Representatives (zastupnički dom), which represents Croatia's 418 local municipalities (opčine).

[34] United States Department of State, *Country Reports on Human Rights Practices for 1992*, (Washington, D.C.: U.S. Government Printing Office, February 1993).

[35] *Ibid.*

[36] Stan Markotich, " Ethnic Serbs in Tudjman's Croatia," *RFE/RL Research Report*, Vol. 2, No. 38, September 24, 1993.

to "represent" the Serbian population, some of whom are listed as political
independents and other whom are members of political parties.[37]

Current estimates indicate that approxiamately 200,000 Serbs fled from
western Slavonia and Krajina during the Croatian Army offensives in mid-1995,
and those Serbs currently remaining in government-controlled areas of Croatia are
believed to comprise only 4 percent of Croatia's population. If a significant
number of Serbs do not return to Croatia or if the Croatian government obstructs
their repatriation,[38] Serbs will no longer be guaranteed proportional respresentation
in parliament. Current proportional respresentation of Serbs in Croatia's

---

[37] The Serbian National Party (Srpska Narodna Stranka - SNS), is one of two political
parties that are devoted specifically to defending Serbian interests in government-controlled
areas of Croatia. Another party representing Serbs in Croatia is led by Zagreb University
philosophy professor Milorad Pupovac. Both Pupovac's party and the SNS work within the
Croatian government system although a third party, the Serbian Democratic Party (Srpska
Demokratska Stranka - SDS), functions in Serbian-controlled areas of Croatia and Bosnia-
Hercegovina. SDS representatives in Croatia initially participated in Croatian politics but
later walked out of the Croatian parliament and were at the forefront of the Serbian rebellion
in Croatia in August 1990 and in Bosnia-Hercegovina in April 1992. Other political parties
in Croatia, such as the Croatian Social Liberal Party (Hrvatska Socijal-Liberalna Stranka -
HSLS), the Social-Democratic Union (Socijaldemokratska Unija - SDU), the Party for
Democratic Change (Stranka Demokratskih Promjena - SDP), the Croatian National Party
(Hrvatksa Narodna Stranka - HNS), and the Party for Social Democratic Action have also
defended the rights of Serbs to varying degrees.

[38] It should be noted that during the Croatian Army offensive in the so-called Krajina
area, President Tudjman issued a message to Serbs in the region calling on them to remain
in their homes and asserting that the Croatian government would "guarantee to the Croatian
Serbs human and ethnic rights within the constitutional and legal order" of Croatia. (See
"President Tudjman's Message to the Croatian Serbs," full text contained in HINA report
of August 4, 1995.) The extent to which Croatia will allow repatriation of Serbs who fled
Krajina remains to be seen. Despite President Tudjman's pronouncement to the contrary,
the burning of Serbian property and villages in Krajina indicates Croatia's unwillingness to
have Serbs return to the area. Eighty-four Serbian refugees who have fled to the FRY and
Bosnian Serb-held territory have asked to be repatriated to western Slavonia and the
Croatian authorities have, in principle, approved their return. Approval from the FRY
authorities has been sought by U.N. officials but, as of August 3, 1995, had not yet been
received. (See United Nations Security Council, "Report of the Secretary-General
Submitted Pursuant to Security Council Resolution 981 (1995)," S/1995/650, 3 August
1995.)

parliament is based on 1991 census figures and guaranteed Serbian representation in parliament in the future remains uncertain.

Although the scope of attacks against Serbs decreased and efforts were made to increase minority representation in parliament between 1992 and 1994, gangs or individual extremists continue to single out Serbian civilians and their property for attack in Croatia apart from any military operation. According to the Croatian government, numerous buildings belonging to Serbs living in Croatia have been damaged or destroyed by explosives, arson or other deliberate means. A total of 7,489 such buildings were damaged or destroyed during 1992, and a total of 220 were destroyed from January to March 1993.[39] The police regularly come to the scene of the crime and write a report. The police claim to investigate the crimes, but the perpetrators are rarely found. According to government sources, by late 1993, criminal proceedings had been initiated against 126 Croats, thirteen Serbs and eight persons belonging to other ethnic groups for the destruction of such property.[40] Although Croatian government agents may not always be responsible for such attacks, prosecution of such crimes continues to be lax.

Although some non-Croats report discrimination in the workplace, most Serbs in Croatia interviewed by Human Rights Watch/Helsinki representatives in the past three years claimed that the denial of citizenship was their main problem. Serbs in the Rijeka area have taken their grievances to the Croatian government in Zagreb and report that they were favorably received and that steps were taken to address some of their concerns. As described in the following section, Serbs are also the main victims of arbitrary evictions by military authorities.

Moreover, the news on state-owned Croatian Television (Hrvatska Televizija - HTV) is often presented in ways which exacerbate rather than ameliorate inter-ethnic strife and discrimination (for example, by exaggerating abuses perpetrated against Croats by Serbian or Muslim forces, or by not reporting or understating abuses perpetrated by Croatian troops.)Publications containing jingoist and rascist materials are published by independent groups in Croatia. Although not directly supported by the government, state-controlled enterprises provide financial aid to these publications by advertising in them. For example, the state-controlled or -managed firms of Croatia Insurance, Tobacco Factory Zadar,

---

[39] U.N. Commission on Human Rights, "Situation of Human Rights in the Territory of the Former Yugoslavia: Fifth periodic report ...," p. 19.

[40] *Ibid.*

Tanker Commerce Zadar, et. al., advertise in *Hrvatski vjesnik*, an independent, right-wing paper based in the town of Vinkovci in eastern Croatia.[41]

In addition to Serbs, other minorities living in Croatia also have been attacked or discriminated against in Croatia, usually in regard to the granting of citizenship. Some have also been mistreated in detention. For example, according to Amnesty International, Džemal Muratovćc was arrested in his home town of Slavonski Brod on February 7, 1994, and allegedly was severely beaten for two days during interrogation. On February 10, he was transferred to another police station in Djakovo and then to the police station in the town of Požega (formerly Slavonska Požega). On February 11, a police doctor visited Muratović and reportedly confirmed injuries consistent with beating, including damage to the kidneys and a burst ear-drum. The doctor recommended a full medical inspection and immediate treatment. Muratović's relatives and lawyer reportedly were not allowed to arrange for their own doctor to examine him.[42]

Muratović, a Croatian citizen of Bosnian Muslim origin, is a truck driver who regularly drove humanitarian aid into Bosnia for a Muslim charity. Muratović and a Croat neighbor who was towing his car after it broke down were arrested together, apparently on suspicion of car theft. The Croat neighbor was released after several hours. Muratović's wife also was brought in for questioning on the first day of his detention and was released after several hours. She and a lawyer subsequently had access to Muratović.[43]

A NOTE ON THE 1995 DECREE ON THE TEMPORARY EXPROPRIATION AND CONTROL OVER CERTAIN PROPERTY

As this report went to print in late August, the Croatian government issued a decree on the Temporary Expropriation and Control Over Certain Property which effectively placed most Serbian-owned property and possessions in Croatia under Croatian government control. The decree, which went into effect on September 4,

---

[41] U.N. Economic and Social Council, Commission on Human Rights, "Situation of human rights in the territory of the former Yugoslavia, Special report on the media, Report of the Special Rapporteur submitted pursuant to Commission resolution 1994/72," E/CN.4/1995/54, December 13, 1994.

[42] Amnesty International Urgent Action, AI Index: EUR 64/01/94, February 14, 1994.

[43] *Ibid.*

1995, places under Croatian government control a) all property "abandoned" by displaced persons from the Krajina and western Slavonia areas, b) property owned but "abandoned" by individuals who left Croatia since August 17, 1990 (the day the Serbian rebellion in Croatia began), c) property owned by individuals residing in the Federal Republic of Yugoslavia (FRY) and the Serbian-controlled areas of eastern Slavonia and Bosnia-Hercegovina, and d) property owned by citizens of the FRY.   Only Serbs who remained in Croatian government-controlled areas throughout the entire war and who hold title to their property are not affected by the decree. Although the decree states that the expropriation of the Serbs' property is "temporary," it does not specify the duration of the government's control over the property.

Such a decree revokes a persons' right to ownership without due process. It punishes all Serbs who remained in "enemy" territory during the war, although they may not have committed any domestic or internationally-recognized crime. Insofar as a person is guilty of a crime, he or she should be held accountable for his or her actions.   Collective punishment of a group because of their ethnicity or residency during war is discriminatory.   Since the Croatian government re-asserted control over the Krajina area in early August 1995, Croats displaced or expelled from Serb-held territory in Bosnia and Croatia and from the FRY are being resettled in homes belonging to Serbs in the Krajina area. Coupled with the destruction of Serbian property and the resettling of Krajina since early August 1995, the new decree collectively punishes Serbs from Krajina and seriously hampers their ability to return to their homes, should they chose to do so in the future.

IV. EVICTIONS FROM STATE-OWNED HOUSING

During communist rule in the former SFRJ, those who were members of the officer corps or worked for the Yugoslav Army (JNA) or any military-owned or operated enterprise (such as military hospitals) were allotted apartments and houses by the Yugoslav Army. Because a majority of the Yugoslav Army's officer corps was Serbian and many of those employed by it in Croatia were non-Croats, the residents of Yugoslav Army-owned apartments in Croatia were primarily non-Croats.

In the past few years, persons residing in apartments formerly owned by the Yugoslav Army have been evicted by members of the Croatian Army, the military police or by unidentified persons in uniform, without recourse to due process. Despite pleas from local human rights and civil liberties groups in Croatia, the government has not taken vigorous steps to provide legal protections to those being evicted nor has the government taken steps to stop and prevent abuse during such evictions. When public pressure against such evictions increases, the military police often refrain temporarily from further evictions. But such evictions resume after protests cease or diminish in frequency.

Human Rights Watch/Helsinki does not take a position on who is entitled to housing owned and operated by the state. We are, however, concerned that state agents are violating the right to due process in such property disputes and are using violence during many evictions. Military authorities should not discriminate by granting or withdrawing housing rights on the basis of ethnicity and/or presumed political views. Nor should military authorities abuse their power by forcefully evicting their perceived "enemies" for the benefit of their perceived friends and allies. The military authorities have also eroded the rule of law in Croatia by refusing to comply with judicial orders restoring housing rights to evicted occupants.

RELEVANT LEGISLATION

The October 1991 Decree
In October 1991, the Croatian government issued a decree transferring the ownership of property belonging to the Yugoslav Army or the Yugoslav Defense Ministry (Savezni Sekretarijat za Narodnu O(d)branu - SSNO) to the Croatian

government. The Croatian Defense Ministry was given the responsibility of managing and administering such property.[44]

The Law Concerning the Temporary Use of Apartments

The fiercest fighting between Croatian troops and Serbian and Yugoslav Army forces occurred during the latter part of 1991, resulting in the displacement of hundreds of thousands of people. Faced with an influx of displaced persons and little housing, the Croatian parliament passed a law allowing for the "temporary use of apartments owned by public enterprises or persons or the Republic of Croatia, that is, [those apartments] over which the Republic of Croatia has the right to use and administer, and which are otherwise empty, vacated or abandoned."[45] The Law Concerning the Temporary Use of Apartments stipulates that the apartments in question are to be used for the housing of displaced persons, refugees and members of the Croatian armed forces and their families.[46] Article 2 allows for the temporary use of the following apartments:

- empty apartments for which no one has obtained tenant rights (*stanarsko pravo*);

---

[44] *Narodne Novine*, Broj 52, October 3, 1991. The October decree was followed by another decree, in December 1991, which stated that ownership of all the property and assets belonging to the former SFRJ was transferred to the Croatian government. (See "Uredbu o preuzimanju sredstava bivše SFRJ u vlasništvo Republike Hrvatske," *Narodne Novine*, Broj 68, December 13, 1991.) The October and December 1991 Croatian government decrees were issued prior to and following, respectively, the signing of an agreement reached between the Croatian government and representatives of the JNA in November and December 1991 regarding the transfer of ownership or use of JNA property to or by the Croatian government and ensuring the safe passage of JNA troops from Croatia. (See "Sporazum" izmedju predstavnici Vlade Republike Hrvatske i Jugoslovenske Narodne Armije (JNA) zaključen u Zagrebu dana 22. novembra/studenog 1991, and "Sporazum o Privremenom Ustupanju Vojne Bolnice u Zagrebu," December 9, 1991.) Both agreements were signed under the auspices of the European Community's Monitoring Mission (ECMM) for the former Yugoslavia.

[45] See Article 1 of the "Zakon o privremenonm korištenju stanova," *Narodne Novine*, Broj 66, December 9, 1991, pp. 2075-79.

[46] *Ibid.*

- vacated apartments for which tenant rights exist and for which it can be determined that the residents of the apartment and members of their household have vacated the premises and removed their belongings; and

- abandoned apartments for which tenant rights exist and for which it can be determined that the residents of the apartment and members of their household have permanently abandoned [their apartments].

The law, therefore, allows the government to utilize apartments formerly owned by the Yugoslav Army or Defense Ministry — commonly referred to as "military apartments" ("*vojni stanovi*" — to house displaced persons and refugees, provided that these apartments are empty or have been vacated. The law does not allow for the use of apartments occupied by persons who have legal ownership of, or hold tenant rights to, the apartment.

The Law Concerning the Temporary Use of Apartments establishes a commission charged with the administration of the apartments in question. The members of this commission include one representative from the Croatian government's Office for Displaced Persons or the Center for Social Welfare. The Croatian Army, the police and the Fund for Housing (*fond za stambene gospodarstva*) each have one representative on the commission.

Former Yugoslav Army-owned apartments which became the property of the Croatian government and over which the Croatian Defense Ministry has control are administered by a commission appointed by the ministry. Similarly, apartments belonging to the Ministry of Interior are administered by a commission appointed by that body. Remaining apartments that are not the property of the Ministries of Defense or Interior are administered by a commission appointed by the Croatian government, on the basis of recommendations offered by the Ministry of Justice and Public Administration. Each of the commissions are to decide how and for whom an apartment is to be allotted on a temporary basis. However, the vast majority of the apartments from which persons are being evicted are administered *de facto* exclusively by the Croatian Army.

Article 9 of the law states that the temporary use of an apartment cannot exceed one year and that, should a displaced person or refugee be able to return to his or her home, the occupier would be required to vacate the apartment. Article 12 makes it a misdemeanor, punishable by a fine, for a person to enter an apartment without a permit from the relevant commission allowing for the temporary use of the apartment. Article 13 of the law requires that the Croatian government establish a commission to monitor and regularly inform the government about the enforcement of the law.

It is important to stress that, according to Croatia's Law Regarding the Temporary Use of Apartments, before an apartment can be allotted to a displaced or other person, the apartment must be empty. The law does not allow for the eviction of persons still living in Yugoslav Army-owned apartments. Indeed, Croatian law expressly states that due process must be afforded to those who face eviction.[48]

Controversy Regarding the Use of Military Apartments After July 24, 1991

In most cases, tenants of apartments formerly owned by the communist state or socialist enterprises have been allowed to buy their apartments and obtain legal ownership, an opportunity which many have taken. However, the tenants of apartments owned by the Croatian government — including apartments formerly owned by the Yugoslav Army or Defense Ministry — generally have not been permitted to purchase, and thereby obtain legal ownership of, their apartments.

Some parts of the Croatian government and legal community — including the Ministry of Defense and local military housing commissions which allot the military apartments to displaced persons and refugees — dispute the right of tenants to reside in military apartments if their tenant rights were issued by the Yugoslav Army after July 1991. They base this on two Croatian government decrees. A July 1991 decree forbade the disposal of real property on the territory of the Republic of Croatia.[49] As described above, the October 1991 decree transferred ownership of property formerly owned by the Yugoslav Army and Defense Ministry to the Croatian government. Both decrees effectively forbid the sale, exchange, donation, transfer of the right to use or administer, leasing and temporary use, mortgage and similar transactions of real estate in Croatia that was previously owned by the former SFRJ.[50] The decrees are seen by some as effectively annulling the rights of tenants if their apartments were allotted by the Yugoslav Army after July 24, 1991; in other words, after July 24, 1991, the transfer of Yugoslav Army-owned property and any action taken by the Yugoslav Army in Croatia is no longer considered valid. Citing these decrees, proponents of this argument claim that the Croatian government has a legal right to evict persons from

---

[48] For a further explanation of such laws, see following section concerning other legislation related to housing.

[49] "Uredba o zabrani raspolaganja nekretninama na teritoriju Republike Hrvatske," *Narodne Novine*, Broj 36, July 24, 1991.

[50] *Ibid.*, See also "Vojna Imovina: Rasetini Lažni Stanovi," *Danas*, April 9, 1993.

military apartments if their tenant rights to the apartment in question were issued after July 24, 1991.

Opponents of the aforementioned position point to internationally-brokered agreements signed by the Croatian government to support their claim that the evictions of persons who received rights to occupy military apartments after July 24, 1991, is illegal. Two agreements negotiated by the European Union (formerly the European Community - EC) are cited to support this position, i.e., the so-called Brioni Declaration signed by Croatia and Slovenia on July 7, 1991, and a November 1991 agreement signed by the Yugoslav Army and the Croatian government.

The Brioni Declaration was signed by Slovenia and Croatia eleven days after both republics declared their independence from the former SFRJ. According to the terms of that agreement, Slovenia and Croatia agreed to suspend, for a period of three months, all declarations and acts passed by the Croatian and Slovenian parliaments that were related to those states' secession from the SFRJ. The Brioni Agreement would allow for the suspension — until October 7, 1991 — of Croatia's July 24, 1991, decree forbidding the transfer and administration of property formerly owned by the Yugoslav Army or Defense Ministry. The suspension of such laws and decrees would ensure that those who obtained tenant rights to military apartments between July 24 and October 7, 1991, could not be evicted by the Croatian government.

Proponents of this argument also assert that, according to Article 4 of the November 22, 1991, agreement between the Yugoslav Army and the Croatian government, the latter agreed "to guarantee the safety and inviolability of private property *and the right to the unhampered use of apartments*" (emphasis added) by members of the JNA who chose not to leave Croatia. The agreement also states that the decision of former Yugoslav Army personnel to remain in Croatia resulted in the termination of their service in the Yugoslav Army and guaranteed them the same civil liberties afforded all other citizens of the Republic of Croatia. In this case, the Croatian government's signature to this agreement forbids the eviction of persons living in military apartments and exempts the application of the July 1991 decree forbidding the transfer of property formerly owned by the SFRJ to tenants of military apartments.

To date, the applicability of the July 1991 decree remains controversial; while some members of the Croatian government cite the decree to justify evictions, others argue that such evictions are illegal.

Other Legislation Related to Housing

Irrespective of whether or not a person retains tenant rights to his or her apartment, Croatia's Law on Housing Relations allows for the revocation of those rights under certain circumstances.[51] For example, Article 99 of the law states that persons may lose the tenant rights to their apartments if they have not lived in the apartment for over six months. However, it is important to note that, according to Article 105 of the Law on Housing Relations, only a court of law can revoke a person's tenant rights; an administrative or government agency — such as the local military housing commissions responsible for the eviction of persons from military apartments — does not have that authority.

The Ministry of Defense often has tried to justify its evictions of persons from "military apartments" by citing amendments to the Law on Housing Relations, which allow for the eviction of persons from their apartments if that person is "an enemy of the state." For example, amendments and revisions to the Law on Housing Relations issued on April 17, 1992, state that a person who has taken part in, or continues to take part in, acts of hostility against the Republic of Croatia, can lose the tenant rights to his or her apartment(s).[52] However, such amendments continue to provide for due process and explicitly state that only a court of law can legally nullify an agreement regarding the use of such a housing unit(s).

ABUSES OF THE LAW

The Croatian Ministry of Defense and local military housing commissions have provided permits allowing soldiers and their families — many of whom are Croats who have been forcibly displaced from their homes in Croatia by rebel Serbian forces — to utilize military apartments despite the fact that the current residents of the apartment — the vast majority of whom are non-Croats and had

---

[51] See section 6, "Prestanak stanarskog prava," of "Zakon o stambenim odnosima," *Narodne Novine*, Broj 51, Zagreb, December 17, 1985. This law was promulgated when Croatia was still part of the former SFRJ. However, the Croatian government has adapted many of the laws of the previous regime either verbatim or with amendments and revisions. A host of laws regulate housing in Croatia. For an index of such laws, refer to Vesna Grubić and Dejan Palić, eds., *Registar važećih pravnih propisa u Republici Hrvatskoj, (Propisi obljavljeni do 21. 3. 1994. (Narodne novine br. 21/94)*, (Zagreb: Informator, 1994), p.20.

[52] See Article 2 of "Zakon o izmjenama i dopunama Zakona o stambenim odnosinma," *Narodne Novine*, Broj 22, April 17, 1992.

formerly been employed by the Yugoslav Army — continue to live in their homes and have not been afforded the opportunity to protest their eviction to an independent arbiter.

In other cases, the local military housing commissions revoke a tenant's rights to occupy a military apartment, despite the fact that only a court of law can rescind such rights. The revocation of a person's tenant rights by the local housing commissions is used to justify his or her eviction. A written notice is sent by the local military housing commission to the tenants in question, notifying them that their right to occupy their military apartment has been rescinded. The notice also specifies the day and time by which they must vacate the premises or be forcibly evicted, usually by Croatian Army soldiers. Threats, harassment, violence and destruction of property often are used by soldiers to force persons from their homes.

The largest number of military apartments in Croatia are located in the cities of Zagreb, Split, Pula, Zadar, Rijeka and Karlovac.[53] In the past three years, Human Rights Watch/Helsinki has received scores of complaints concerning forcible evictions in all of the aforementioned cities. The victims of such evictions are predominantly non-Croats, most often Serbs. Croats whose family members — usually non-Croats — had worked for the Yugoslav Army but had left Croatia also are being evicted from their homes. We have documented several cases involving the excessive use of force during evictions, were present at an illegal eviction and have spoken with government officials about these practices. Croatian human rights organizations, such as the Croatian Helsinki Committee for Human Rights and the Center for Peace, Non-Violence and Human Rights, have worked tirelessly on this issue and have documented scores of additional cases.[54] The following select cases illustrate the methods used by the Croatian Army and the military housing commissions to illegally evict persons from their homes.

---

[53] "Otkupiti se može oko 60 posto fonda," *Vjesnik*, March 24, 1993. According to the press report, a total of 28,340 military apartments exist in these aforementioned cities. Approximately 700 such military apartments are located in what were then Serbian-controlled parts of Croatia.

[54] On November 2-3, 1994, the Croatian Helsinki Committee for Human Rights organized a forum with non-governmental and governmental representatives to discuss the problem of illegal evictions in Croatia. Statements made by conference participants are contained in Hrvatski Helsinški Odbor za Ljudska Prava, *Deložacije u Republici Hrvatskoj: Pravni, Etički i Socijalni Aspekti*, Zagreb, December 1994.

Case #1:

Evictions from state-owned housing are most frequent in Zagreb and Split. Between February and November 1993, 364 illegally evicted persons or families appealed to the courts in Split.[55] The courts ruled on 280 cases, in which all but 60 of those evicted were reinstated in their homes. However, according to the U.N. Special Rapporteur, the military authorities in Split have refused to execute almost all of the court orders.[56] The offices of two lawyers who defended the evicted tenants were damaged by explosives planted by allegedly unknown assailants.

The attempted eviction of a mother and her daughter in Split resulted in the death of a bodyguard they had hired to protect them. V.P. and her mother — both Croats — are the daughter and wife of a former Yugoslav Army officer — a Serb — who left Croatia in late August 1991 when the Yugoslav Army was withdrawing from Croatia.[57] After Mr. P. had left Croatia, the P. family was harassed[58] and Croatian military personnel in uniform repeatedly threatened Mr. P.'s wife, daughter and son with eviction. Ms. P. and her daughter were frequently visited, interrogated and sometimes threatened by Croatian military personnel in uniform during the course of two years.

According to Ms. P. and her daughter, members of the fourth battalion of the Croatian Army had come to their apartment building on the 26th or 27th of July 1993, compiling a list of persons who lived in the apartment building. According to Ms. P.:

> All the apartments in the building are military apartments ...
> They [the soldiers compiling the list] wanted to know how many

---

[55] U.N. Commission on Human Rights, "Situation of Human Rights in the Territory of the Former Yugoslavia: Sixth periodic report on the situation of human rights in the territory of the former Yugoslavia submitted by Mr. Tadeusz Mazowiecki, Special Rapporteur of the Commission on Human Rights, pursuant to paragraph 32 of Commission resolution 1993/7 of 23 February 1993," E/CN.4/1994/110, February 21, 1994, p. 17.

[56] *Ibid.*

[57] Although V.P. is the daughter of a Croatian mother and a Serbian father, she identified herself as a Croat at the time of our interview.

[58] In early October 1991, their car was sprayed with graffiti and the tires were slashed. V.P. claimed that their telephone was arbitrarily disconnected and that their efforts to re-connect the telephone for two years were in vain. V.P. and her mother said that their telephone had been re-connected only several days before our interview.

people lived in each apartment. They went only to the Serbs'
homes and to the homes of those persons who had left [Croatia]
with the JNA [but whose families remained in Split]. These
soldiers were not people from Split. They were from
Hercegovina.[59]

According to V.P., Ms. P.'s daughter:

Once they came by when only my brother — who is twenty
years old — was at home. They didn't have a warrant to search
the place. They searched the dresser, and they said my mother
had to come to the police station.

Ms. P. and V.P. went to the police station the following day but V.P. was
not allowed to enter the room with her mother. According to Ms. P.:

They told me I wasn't a good Croat; otherwise I would have sent
my son into the Croatian Army. Two men questioned me. They
were dressed in civilian clothing and they identified themselves
only after I insisted. I demanded to see the chief of the station,
and then they told me that I could leave. I was never bothered by
them again.

On Tuesday, August 10, 1993, while V.P. and her mother were on
vacation, Mladen Šunjić, a member of the fourth battalion of the Croatian Army,
came to their apartment, removed their name from the door and replaced it with a
notice stating "Do not enter — dangerous." Ms. P.'s neighbors called the police, but
Šunjić had already left by the time the police arrived. V.P. and her mother returned
from vacation on Saturday, August 14, but they went to the police before returning
to their apartment. V.P. recounted their experience with the civilian and military
police on that day:

We went to the first police station and spoke with Mr. Jure
Catipović, the deputy commander of the station. He called the
military police. The civilian police escorted us to our apartment

---

[59] Hercegovina is the southwestern region of Bosnia-Hercegovina. Most of western
Hercegovina is overwhelmingly populated by Croats and many Croats from this area joined
the Croatian Army, especially during the war in Croatia in 1991.

building in a police car, and we waited for the military police to arrive. It was about 9:00 in the morning. We went to the apartment with the military police, and we knocked on the door. Šunjić was alone in the apartment. He was stripped to the waist but had a gun strapped to his belt. He wouldn't let us into the apartment and told the military police officer that he wasn't going to do anything he told him to do.

Ms. P. continued:

The military police didn't want to argue with him so they took all of us, including Šunjić, to the military police station at Lora,[60] where we went to meet the commander of the military police. The civilian police officers then left. The commander wasn't there so we were taken to [see] the officer on duty. After we spoke to him, Šunjić went in to be questioned but he obviously knew everyone there — they were friends. He didn't stay inside longer than two minutes. Then they questioned us about things that had nothing to do with the apartment. They asked where we were from, about my husband. We eventually asked about the status of our apartment, and they asked me if it was a military apartment. I replied that it was. They told me that he [i.e., Šunjić] had more right to be there than we.

We left the room and asked to speak to the commander but they said he wasn't in, that it was a Saturday. We left, intending to go back to the civilian police, at which point we saw soldiers driving Šunjić somewhere — we presumed back to our apartment. We went to the civilian police and explained that the military police wouldn't do anything to help us. They were surprised but said that they could not do anything — that Šunjić was a soldier and they could only help us if he attacked us.

V.P. and her mother went to her grandmother's and later in the afternoon returned to the military police headquarters at Lora. According to Ms. P.:

---

[60] Lora is the name of a port in Split. Formerly the site of a former JNA military base, it is now used by the Croatian armed forces.

We spoke to a higher-ranking officer, and he asked me for the document giving me the right to occupy my apartment, which was issued twenty years ago. He told me that it was no longer valid. Then he told me that they couldn't do anything until the military court interviewed us.

At about 7:00 p.m., we went to the city court, which is a civilian court. We spoke with the judge on duty. She was good to us, but she told us that this was not within her jurisdiction and told us that we had to go to the military court. She referred us to a lawyer.

Ms. P. and her daughter returned to their apartment in the evening. The military police came twice to their apartment although neither Ms. P. nor her daughter had called them. According to Ms. P.:

At about 9:00 p.m., we returned to our apartment, and we told the [civilian] police that we were there. They came five minutes later to write a report. While the two police officers were still there, two military police officers arrived. It was about 10:00 or 10:30 p.m.. We had not called the military police, so they left. After the civilian police officers left, three military police officers arrived, at about 10:45 p.m.. They had long-barrelled weapons, but I wouldn't let them into the apartment.

In the interim, V.P. had called a private agency, called "Bond," asking for a bodyguard. The bodyguard, Maksimilian Marković, arrived several minutes before the three military police officers. Marković opened the door and invited the three military police officers to have a seat in the apartment. According to V.P.:

We described to the military police officers what had happened with the apartment, who my father was, and the three military police officers were very polite. They left shortly thereafter. Marković stayed, and he went to fix the lock on our door; we had to break it to get into the apartment because Šunjić had replaced our lock with his.

While Ms. P., her daughter and the bodyguard were in the apartment, Šunjić broke in. According to V.P.:

[Marković] had finished the lock at about 12:15 a.m.. Because they were rationing electricity[61], he came into the living room with two candles ... and asked for some water, which [my mother] got from the kitchen. It was then that Šunjić came and kicked in the door. He had a huge gun, plus another gun in his holster. He came to us in the living room and started yelling what we were doing in his apartment! Marković told him that there was no need to yell or to get upset. He told [Šunjić] that he'd explain everything to him. He showed him all our documents. Šunjić then told Marković, "What kind of Croat are you!?! I kill your kind with two fingers. The Četniks[62] burned three of my houses!"

While he was arguing, my mother and I sneaked out of the apartment and ran across the street to some friends' home to call the police, but we heard shots coming out of the apartment. I ran into the apartment to see what had happened. Šunjić went toward the hallway, and we went after him and he asked me where his lock was. I told him I didn't know. He told Maks to get the phone and call the military police. Maks told Šunjić to call them himself at which point Šunjić shot off a round of bullets into the floor, about half a meter from us. He started yelling and told us to get out. I said OK, and I ran outside barefoot, and then I heard another burst of gunfire which lasted for about thirty or forty seconds. I ran across the street to call the Bond agency.

---

[61] Much of the Dalmatian coast was supplied with water and electricity from dams and power plants in the Dalmatian hinterland, most of which was controlled by rebel Serbian forces between August 1990 and August 3, 1995. Rebel Serbian forces shut off the water and electricity supply to Croatian government-controlled areas of Dalmatia and, as a result, much of the Dalmatian coast had to ration water and electricity at varying times in recent years.

[62] Četnik forces loyal to the Serbian king fought against Croatian fascists (known as Ustašas) and Tito's communist partisans during World War II. The Četniks were known for their brutality against non-Serbs and Serbs opposed to their policies. Serbian forces currently fighting in Croatia and Bosnia often are referred to as "Četniks" by Croats, Muslims and some Serbs opposed to their policies.

The second burst of gunfire killed Marković. V.P.'s mother had been waiting for the police to arrive outside the apartment building after her daughter ran back into the apartment when she heard the first gunshots. According to V.P.:

> Two civilian police officers arrived quickly. The military police came after they did. They disarmed Šunjić, and the military police took him away. While they were doing this, they wanted to take us to Lora for questioning, but I refused and told them that I would come in the morning. They finished filing their report at 3:00 a.m., and the military police told us that no one could sleep in the apartment so, at 3:00 a.m., we walked for an hour and a half to my grandmothers's. We didn't want anyone to drive us.

V.P. and her mother went to the military police on Monday, after consulting with a lawyer who instructed them to go to the military police. After they gave their statement to the military police, Ms. P. and her daughter went to the military court, where they also gave a statement to a Mr. B.,[63] who promised to accompany them to their apartment the next day. Nevertheless, Ms. P. and her daughter had not returned to their apartment at the time of our interview.

V.P. and her mother reported that Šunjić was in jail and that he had been charged with murder. Human Rights Watch/Helsinki has not been able to confirm whether Šunjić was convicted and if, he had been found guilty, whether and where he was serving a sentence of imprisonment. According to Ms. P. and her daughter, Šunjić was originally from Mostar, Bosnia-Hercegovina, but belonged to the fourth battalion of the Croatian Army.

Although the Croatian authorities properly arrested and charged Šunjić, local military police officers appear to have been in complicity with Šunjić in his efforts to remove the P. family forcibly from their home. Indeed, this is a pattern found throughout Croatia — local military commanders encourage or condone forcible evictions by soldiers, and often such evictions are characterized by a lack of due process, discrimination, violence and, in this case, murder.

The murdered bodyguard, Maksimilian Marković was twenty-one years old, married to an eighteen-year-old woman and the father of an eighteen-month-old son. He was a Croat by nationality and had served throughout Dalmatia as a member of the 72nd and 73rd Split brigade of the military police of the Croatian Army. After his death, Marković's father, mother and brother wrote an open letter

---

[63] Ms. P. and her daughter asked that the name of the man not be disclosed.

to members of the fourth Split brigade of the Croatian Army, to which Mladen Šunjić — Marković's murderer — had belonged. The letter was published in the Split-based daily *Slobodna Dalmacija*.[64] In the letter, Marković's family demanded to know from the fourth battalion why it had not taken steps to prevent the "terrorization" of Ms. P. and her daughter. The family condemned the fact that officials of the Croatian Army — including then Croatian Army Chief of Staff General Janko Bobetko — and members of the fourth battalion did not publicly condemn the murder of their son and brother. The family ended their letter by asking the Croatian Army to take measures to ensure that similar tragedies be prevented in the future.

Case #2:
Arbitrary violence is frequently used by Croatian Army soldiers or the military police in many illegal evictions. In some cases, human rights activists working to prevent evictions have been the target of such attacks. On February 2, 1994, the president of the Split-based Dalmatian Committee for Human Rights was severely beaten by uniformed men while trying to prevent an illegal eviction. The attack occurred in the presence of the military and civilian police, which reportedly did not intervene to stop the attack.[65]

Members of the Dalmatian Committee for Human Rights report that they were physically attacked twice in Split by the same Croatian Army soldier in mid- and late February 1994. The soldier reportedly had moved into an apartment illegally. According to the Dalmatian Committee for Human Rights, on February 26, Mr. Rogošić, a member of the Committee, was severely beaten and kicked by the aforementioned soldier in a cafe. Rogošić fainted as a result of the beating, and the attacker eventually was stopped by persons accompanying him.[66] To the best of our knowledge, charges were never brought against the soldier who beat Mr. Rogošić.

---

[64] "Osramoćeno Vitežštvo," *Slobodna Dalmacija*, August 21, 1993.

[65] U.N. Commission on Human Rights, "Situation of Human Rights in the Territory of the Former Yugoslavia: Sixth periodic report...," p. 18. See also Letter from Dalmatian Committee for Human Rights (Dalmatinski Komitet za Ljudska Prava) to Croatian Defense Minister Gojko Šušak, March 22, 1994.

[66] Letter from Dalmatian Committee for Human Rights (Dalmatinski Komitet za Ljudska Prava) to Croatian Defense Minister Gojko Šušak, March 22, 1994.

Case #3:

Some evictions have also been accompanied by the use of force against members of the media, thereby obstructing freedom of the press. For example, foreign journalists covering the eviction of a family in Zagreb on December 3, 1993, were prevented by Croatian Army soldiers and members of the military police from approaching the apartment complex in which the family lived. The soldiers attacked a journalist for the Associated Press, "tugging her by the hair and throwing her to the ground." A video cassette was confiscated from a television crew, and a camera operator was struck in the face. Apparently in response to protests from the international community, the Croatian Defense Ministry later ceased its efforts to evict the residents of the apartment in question.[67]

Case #4:

In 1993, a Human Rights Watch/Helsinki representative and domestic human rights activists arrived at the home of a couple who were being evicted by Croatian Army soldiers in the Dugave section of Zagreb. Ms. I.D., who retained the rights to occupy the apartment, and her husband had worked at the Yugoslav Army's military hospital in Zagreb and were allotted their apartment as its employees. After the Yugoslav Army left Croatia, Mr. and Ms. D. decided to remain in Zagreb and continued to work at the hospital, which has been renamed "New Hospital" (Nova Bolnica). Mr. and Ms. D. received three notices that they were to be evicted by the local military housing commission. Anticipating violence and threats, Mr. and Ms. D. sent their two children to live with relatives in another part of Zagreb.

On June 10, 1993, approximately ten Croatian Army soldiers armed with handguns came to the apartment. Ms. D. asserted that the soldiers arrived in two trucks and with a written order for their eviction. Ms. D. claims that the soldiers verbally threatened her and her husband, demanding that they leave the apartment. According to Ms. D., two civilian police officers arrived at the same time as the Croatian Army soldiers, and the police officers ordered the soldiers to remain outside, claiming that the military did not have jurisdiction to deal with civilians. The soldiers complied and, at the time of our arrival, were standing outside the building and allowed us to enter the apartment. The two police officers remained in the apartment.

---

[67] "Croatia: Report of Croatian Army Assault Against Foreign Journalists," International Freedom of Expression Exchange citing the British Broadcasting Corporation (BBC), December 10, 1993, and "Croatia: Soldiers Assault Journalists Covering Tenant Eviction," International Freedom of Expression Exchange, December 13, 1993.

Local human rights advocates were in the apartment with Mr. and Ms. D.. These activists had contacted the office of Stipe Mesić, then the president of the Croatian parliament and an opponent of such evictions, asking him to intercede on behalf of Mr. and Ms. D.. Mesić and Ante Djapić, a member of the parliament's human rights committee, sent a fax to officials at the Ministry of Defense demanding that they halt the eviction. Two unarmed representatives of the local military housing commission — dressed in civilian clothing — then arrived at the apartment to reiterate that Mr. and Ms. D. must leave the apartment. After about two hours of telephone and fax communication between Mesić and the Defense Ministry, an order was sent to stop the eviction.

A military police officer named Mario Marković then arrived and asked to enter the home. He politely interviewed the couple, specifically asking if the soldiers had mistreated them in any way. They responded that they were threatened with force by the soldiers if they did not move out. Mr. Marković recorded their statements and asked for the names of the soldiers standing outside. Some of the soldiers had already left, but others gave their names to Marković. Marković, the two representatives from the housing commission and the police officers then wrote up their reports, exchanged papers and left.

In this instance, the eviction of Mr. and Ms. D. was prevented because high-ranking government officials had interceded at the request of local human rights groups, specifically the Center for Peace, Non-Violence and Human Rights and the Human Rights Commission of the Social-Democratic Union (Socijaldemokratska Unija - SDU).[68] The behavior of the two civilian officers and Mario Marković, the military police officer, was commendable. However, the Croatian Army soldiers and the representatives of the local military housing commission were rude and insulting and, at first, had dismissed the authority of high-ranking government officials to dispute decrees of the military authorities.

Although Mr. and Ms. D. were not evicted at that time, Ms. D. was sure that they would be evicted at a later date. Indeed, in November 1993, Mr. and Ms. D. were evicted from their home. Mr. and Ms. D. have appealed to the courts.

Case #5:

According to the U.N. Special Rapporteur, proceedings had been initiated against "enemies of the state" in 3,120 instances by November 1993, under amendments and revisions to the Law on Apartment Relations, which allows for

---

[68] The SDU is a left-of-center political party in Croatia.

the termination of tenant rights to such persons, pending a court hearing.[69] In many instances, as in the following case documented by local human rights groups in Osijek, non-Croats are summarily evicted from their homes under the pretext that they, or members of their family, are "enemies of the state." They are not afforded the right to due process, although Croatian law guarantees them that right.

According to an ordinance issued by the local military housing commission in Osijek, M.V. was required to leave his apartment and temporarily move into a smaller apartment "which would accommodate the number of persons in his family." The ordinance stated that spacious military apartments were being confiscated from families whose members had joined rebel Serbian forces and who had left behind other family members to care for their property. The ordinance stated that, until a decree specifying the status of such family members was established, the apartment in question was to be used to house refugees and displaced persons; family members currently occupying the apartment would be moved to a smaller military or publicly-owned apartment. Should the refugees or displaced persons return to their homes and vacate the apartment in question, the ability of the original occupants to return to the apartment would again be considered.[70]

The fact or suspicion that a member of a family is fighting with rebel Serbian forces does not allow for the persecution of family members who have not participated in such hostilities and or broken any laws. The eviction of such persons from their home places guilt on persons by virtue of their association with a member of their family. Insofar as a person is guilty of a crime, the individual in question — and not his or her family members — should be held accountable before a court of law.

Also, the ordinance in question was applied to evict M.V. and his family without legal basis. In fact, the ordinance explicitly states that a law regulating the status of families whose members had joined rebel Serbian forces, but whose other members remained in Croatian government-controlled areas, had not yet been issued. In the absence of a court ruling, a local military housing commission does not have the right to evict a family summarily.

---

[69] U.N. Commission on Human Rights, "Situation of Human Rights in the Territory of the Former Yugoslavia: Fifth periodic report...," p. 18.

[70] Human Rights Watch/Helsinki retains a copy of this and similar ordinances issued by the Osijek military housing commission. The name and document number of the person in question has not been disclosed to protect the person's identity.

Case #6:

In some cases, persons who have been illegally evicted from their homes seek redress in court and obtain a ruling in their favor, ordering the return of the evicted tenants to their apartments. However, some local military housing commissions and military police officers refuse to respect the ruling of the courts. In his report, the U.N. Special Rapporteur stated that his field staff

> had received an official notice dated July 20, 1993, in which the registrar of the Municipal Court of Rijeka testifies that 'the execution of the court order [to reinstate the unlawfully evicted tenant] was not acted upon because the military police did not obey the writ given by the court' on the grounds that they 'have different orders from their superiors.'[71]

Human Rights Watch/Helsinki has documented a similar case in Osijek. During the shelling of Osijek in 1991, B.B. and his wife, L. — both Croats — left Osijek to stay with relatives in Germany. In early February 1992, during the family's absence from Osijek, M.S, a Croatian Army soldier broke into the B.'s apartment, changed the lock on their door and moved in with his family. M.S. and his family had been forcibly displaced from their home in the village of Laslovo by rebel Serbian forces in 1991 or early 1992 and were living in Osijek as displaced persons.[72]

When B.B. and his wife returned to Osijek, they asked M.S. to move out of their apartment but he refused. B.B. then filed a claim with the local Secretariat for Housing and Urban Affairs demanding that M.S. move out of their apartment within twenty-five days, as specified by Article 94 of the Law on Housing Relations. In the interim, M.S. sought and obtained from the military housing commission a permit to use the B.'s apartment for a period of one year. The Ministry of Justice and Public Administration declared invalid M.S.'s permit, but

---

[71] U.N. Commission on Human Rights, "Situation of Human Rights in the Territory of the Former Yugoslavia: Fifth periodic report ...," p. 18.

[72] The information contained in this section is taken from a letter written by B.B. and his wife describing their predicament and from documents from the constitutional court of Croatia, Osijek's Secretariat for Urban Affairs, Construction and Communal Housing Issues, the Ministry of Justice and Public Administration and other related documents. Human Rights Watch/Helsinki representatives interviewed M.S. in July 1993 and his account of the events confirmed the details of the B.'s letter contained in this section.

the local military housing commission refused to revoke the permit and M.S. remained in the B.'s apartment.

In June 1992, B.B. and his wife appealed their case to Croatia's constitutional court, which agreed with the Ministry of Justice and ruled that the issuance of the local military housing commission's permit had been illegal. Despite the ruling of Croatia's highest court, the military housing commission still refused to revoke M.S.'s permit.

Human Rights Watch/Helsinki spoke with M.S. in July 1993, at which point he continued to occupy the B.'s apartment. M.S. was politically active in Osijek at the time of our visit, lobbying for the rights of displaced persons to housing. M.S. insisted that he had a right to the B.'s apartment by virtue of his affiliation with the Croatian Army and claimed that he had been assured, presumably by the authorities, that he would not be removed from the apartment. M.S.'s main concern focused on returning to his home in Laslovo.

Branimir Glavaš, the governor (župan) of the Baranja, eastern Slavonia and Srijem regions, and Petar Kljajić, the head of Osijek's military housing commission and president of the Osijek district (okružni) court, support — and Kljajić is directly responsible for — the evictions of persons from "military apartments" in Osijek. Both men reject the claim that such evictions are illegal. When Human Rights Watch/Helsinki representatives inquired about M.S.'s right to remain in the B.'s apartment, both Glavaš and Kljajić[73] defended M.S.'s right to remain in the apartment. Kljajić insisted that, as head of the housing commission that had allowed M.S. to make use of the B.'s apartment, he would do nothing to remove M.S. and his family from the apartment in question. Glavaš implied that the B.'s had been "cowards" when they left Osijek and that those who remained in Osijek — particularly those who fought to defend the city, as had M.S. — had priority to housing. Although Glavaš claimed that B.B. and his family could eventually return to their apartment, he said that they would have to wait until M.S. was ready to leave. According to Glavaš:

> I don't care what you human rights types think. I have soldiers who were kicked out of their houses by the Serb[ian forces], who fought bravely and defended the city while it was being attacked. They and their families had no place to live so we put them in the apartments and houses of those who left Osijek during its most difficult days. Now these cowards who left the city are coming back, and they want their houses and apartments

---

[73] Interviewed in Osijek in July 1993.

back. I don't care who these people [who are returning] happen to be — I don't care if they're Serbs, Hungarians, Croats or whatever. I'm not going to kick out the soldiers who stayed here to fight to accommodate those who left Osijek and spent their time drinking in European cafes during the war and who now want to come back. They'll have to wait until we can find the soldiers and the displaced persons a decent place to live.

Glavaš's response is not unique; it is typical of residents who remained and continue to live in areas most affected by the war, particularly in the municipalities of Osijek, Karlovac, Pakrac, Slavonski Brod, Gospić, Ogulin, Zadar, Šibenik and Dubrovnik. The need to care for displaced persons and refugees and the need to provide housing for soldiers and their families who otherwise do not have a home is a necessary task and hardship for the Croatian authorities, particularly the local authorities in the aforementioned areas. However, the eviction without basis in law of those formerly associated with the Yugoslav Army, those who fled their homes temporarily during the war and others is not a justifiable means through which authorities can provide housing for refugees and displaced persons.

PROTESTS BY HUMAN RIGHTS GROUPS AND THE GOVERNMENT'S RESPONSE

The Osijek, Zagreb and Rijeka chapters of Croatia's Center for Peace, Non-Violence and Human Rights, representatives of the human rights committee of the Social-Democratic Union (SDU), the Croatian Helsinki Committee for Human Rights and local human rights advocates in Split have worked arduously for over three years in an effort to prevent arbitrary evictions in their respective municipalities and throughout the country. In numerous letters to the Croatian president and parliamentary president, Croatia's Roman Catholic archbishop, Franjo Kuharić, also has protested against evictions of families from state-owned housing. Moderate, liberal, and even some conservative members of the Croatian government and ruling party have protested the role of the military police in forcing the eviction of tenants from housing formerly owned by the Yugoslav Army or the Yugoslav Defense Ministry.

On February 12, 1993, Stjepan Herceg, then Croatia's State Prosecutor, sent a letter to Mate Laušić, the chief of the military police, protesting the abusive behavior of, and forcible evictions by, members of the military police. The letter states that only the courts can decide whether or not a person has the right to occupy an apartment or dwelling and that the military police do not have the legal or other authority to evict persons forcibly from their homes. The letter asks Laušić to ensure that the military police respect law and order.[74]

While some members of the Croatian government have been sympathetic and have intervened to prevent such evictions, often their successes are only temporary. Sooner or later, members of the Croatian Army or the military police arrive and evict the apartment's tenants. The Ministry of Defense and local military housing commissions have turned a deaf ear to the efforts of human rights groups and even some high-ranking members of the Croatian government.

In July 1994, the presence of human rights activists and foreign journalists prevented the Croatian police and soldiers from serving eviction notices on two families, who are Croatian by nationality.[75] Indeed, due to the work of local human rights groups in Croatia, many evictions have been postponed. However, some human rights workers who have peacefully protested such evictions and have remained on the premises while evictions were in progress have been arrested and interrogated, and some have been beaten. On September 27, 1994, members of local non-governmental organizations[76] and other persons were severely beaten by the police during an eviction.[77]

Tensions are high between the various groups involved. In some cases, displaced persons have illegally broken into apartments which residents had temporarily evacuated to wait out the war in Croatia. In other instances, local housing commissions are granting permits to those displaced persons who broke into the apartments, legalizing their illegal entrance after the fact. In still other instances, displaced persons who had illegally broken into an apartment are evicted

---

[74] Letter from Stjepan Herceg, State Prosecutor of the Republic of Croatia, to Mate Laušić, Chief of Military Police, Defense Ministry of the Republic of Croatia, Zagreb, February 12, 1993. The letter is listed as No. A-38/93 and was sent from the Office of the State Prosecutor of the Republic of Croatia. Human Rights Watch/Helsinki retains a copy of the letter in its files.

[75] Reuters report of July 11, 1994, as summarized in *Radio Free Europe/Radio Liberty Daily Report*, July 12, 1994, p.5.

[76] The following human rights organizations were present during the eviction: the Anti-War Campaign Center for Peace, Non-Violence and Human Rights, the Group for Human Rights Direct Help, the Croatian Helsinki Committee for Human Rights, and Dom.

[77] United Nations Security Council, Annex to "Human Rights Questions: Human Rights Situations...," p. 25.

and sent to collective centers for displaced persons and refugees, where accommodations are not as comfortable as in a private apartment.[78] Further cases involve evictions of refugees and displaced persons who have fled rebel Serbian-occupied areas and received apartments via friends or in apartment-swaps. These persons are evicted despite the fact that the law on Displaced Persons and Refugees[79] forbids their eviction unless alternate housing can be provided.

Despite the tensions, many displaced persons and refugees with whom we spoke did not approve of the evictions of former JNA personnel or of other refugees and displaced persons and did not feel secure in the temporary apartments in which they lived. According to a man who had been displaced from his home in eastern Slavonia and was currently living in an apartment from which the tenant had been forcibly evicted in Osijek:[80]

> We have problems with housing in this city. There are many displaced persons who were kicked out of their homes in 1991 and 1992 by Serbian forces and others continue to be expelled from their homes in [Serbian-controlled areas of] Baranja and eastern Slavonia. Just fifteen days ago, another ten people were expelled from Baranja — they're in Čepin now. We need housing. If we don't have housing they start kicking people out of their homes. Those of us who live in these apartments [from which people have been evicted] don't feel any safer. We don't want to leave the apartment because you never know who'll move in while we've gone to buy milk or run an errand.

By the end of 1993, the Croatian authorities had assumed control of approximately 2,000 apartments that formerly belonged to the Yugoslav Army, effectively rendering homeless many of the apartments' former occupants.[81] In June 1994, President Tudjman told veterans of the war in Croatia that they were entitled to housing, suggesting this could be provided at the expense of those living in so-

---

[78] For example, see "Rat stambenom kaosu!," *Glas Slavonije*, January 29, 1993.

[79] *Narodne Novine*, No. 96/93.

[80] Interviewed by Human Rights Watch/Helsinki representatives on July 12, 1993, in Osijek.

[81] *Ibid.*

called "military apartments," most of whom are non-Croats. According to press reports, President Tudjman was quoted as saying: "Let us prove we are a civilized people, that we will grant all ethnic and minority rights to Serbs who accept Croatia as their homeland. [But] why are there 6,000 apartments with Serbs inside and you, Croatian invalids [i.e., veterans handicapped as a result of the war], haven't got any?"[82]

Tadeusz Mazowiecki, the U.N. Special Rapporteur, met with Defense Ministry officials in August and December 1993 to convey his concerns about the illegal evictions. On both occasions, he was assured that steps would be taken to improve the situation. During his meeting in December 1993, the Special Rapporteur was informed that

> a moratorium had been adopted as of December 10 whereby all evictions would cease for a 20-day period, during which time all individual cases, as well as [relevant] legislation.., would be examined. The Special Rapporteur was also informed that the Ministry of Defense was prepared to undertake concrete measures to compensate those who had been affected by the illegal evictions. Furthermore, the Special Rapporteur was informed that a Commission of Control has been established in order to regulate the activities of the Housing Commission established pursuant to the Law on the Provisional Use of Apartments of 4 December 1994.[83]

Following the December 1993 moratorium, reports of evictions decreased. Toward the end of 1993, some local authorities, such as those of the city council of Pula, decided to stop all evictions until the Administrative Court of Croatia ruled on the lawfulness of each individual case.[84]

The U.N. Special Rapporteur reported that between March and mid-1994 his staff had not received reports of evictions carried out by Croatian Army soldiers

---

[82] *Ibid.*

[83] U.N. Commission on Human Rights, "Situation of Human Rights in the Territory of the Former Yugoslavia: Sixth periodic report ...," p. 17.

[84] U.N. Commission on Human Rights, "Situation of Human Rights in the Territory of the Former Yugoslavia: Fifth periodic report ... " p. 18.

on active duty.[85] By late 1994, the Special Rapporteur's staff was primarily investigating evictions involving soldiers on active duty which took place prior to March 1994. However, the staff pointed out that although evictions in 1994 decreased, those soldiers responsible for forced or illegal evictions in the past have not been disciplined nor criminally prosecuted for their abuses. Despite Croatian government promises to do so, no financial compensation has been provided to. victims of illegal and forced evictions.[86] Moreover, as illustrated in the preceding cases, forcible evictions continue in 1995.

In mid-1994, the Croatian government accepted a draft proposal for a law regulating evictions from state-owned housing, but parliament postponed indefinately a vote on the proposal. According to the proposal, the occupants of state-owned apartments that were allotted to them before October 1991 would have the right to buy the apartment. According to the Special Rapporteur, the law does not appear to provide guarantees for the legal tenants.[87] The Croatian government also promised to create a Commission of Control that would regulate the activities of the military housing commission but the Special Rapporteur had not been informed of the commission's work as of November 1994.[88]

On November 22, 1994, the Special Rapporteur was informed by the Croatian Foreign Ministry that Croatia's constitutional court had ruled on July 7, 1993, and March 30, 1994, to confirm the constitutionality and legality of the Decree on the Prohibition of Free Disposal of Real Estate in the Territory of the Republic of Croatia and other relevant decrees of July 24, 1991, and October 2, 1991.[89] The consitutional court has also agreed to review, but as of January 1995

---

[85] United Nations Security Council, Annex to "Human Rights Questions: Human Rights Situations ..." p. 25.

[86] *Ibid.*

[87] United Nations Security Council, Annex to "Human Rights Questions: Human Rights Situations ...," p. 26.

[88] *Ibid.*

[89]U.N. Economic and Social Council, Commission on Human Rights, "Situation of human rights in the territory of the former Yugoslavia: Tenth periodic report on the situation of human rights in the territory of the former Yugoslavia submitted by Mr. Tadeusz Mazowiecki, Special Rappporteur of the Commission on Human Rights, pursuant to paragraph 37 of Commission resolution 1994/72 of 9 March 1994," E/CN.4/1995/57, January 16, 1995, p. 13. See preceding section of this report concerning relevant legislation

has not yet ruled on, the constitutionality and applicability of article 94 of the 1985 housing law, which has been used as a basis for forcible evictions without a court decision.[90] Following a November 1994 symposium on forced evictions sponsored by the Croatian Helsinki Committee for Human Rights and attended by Croatian government officials, non-governmental organizations and other interested parties, administrative organs of the government decided to stop the evictions based on the July 24, 1991, regulations, until the issue was taken up in parliament.[91]

Currently, approximately 15,000 occupants of state-owned apartments face eviction. Despite government promises to the contrary, forcible evictions continue in Croatia.

---

pertaining to forced evictions from state-owned property for an explanation of the July 14, 1991, and October 2, 1991, decrees.

[90] *Ibid.*

[91] *Ibid.*

V. TREATMENT OF REFUGEES

THE SITUATION OF REFUGEES IN CROATIA

Attacks against and harassment of Muslim refugees escalated in 1993 but have since subsided. Most of the attacks against Muslim refugees were due to hostility felt against Muslims who fought Bosnian Croat forces in central Bosnia throughout 1993. In early 1994, a rapprochement between Bosnian Croats and Muslims, on the one hand, and the Republics of Croatia and Bosnia-Hercegovina on the other, decreased tensions between Muslims and Croats in general. In recent months, conciliatory press coverage and government statements have led to a decrease in attacks against Muslim refugees in Croatia. However, following the expulsion of Bosnian Croats and Muslims from their homes in the Bosnian Serb-held city of Banja Luka in August 1995, the Croatian government has reportedly been allowing Croats to enter Croatia but has only accepted a small number of Muslims, most of whom remain on the Croatian-Bosnian border. Also in August 1995, the Croatian government was obstructing deliverance of humanitarian aid to rebel Muslims loyal to Fikret Abdić, a renegade leader aligned with the Bosnian and Croatian Serbs against Bosnian-government forces in the Bihać area.

The fighting between Croats and Muslims in central Bosnia in 1993 resulted in the displacement of hundreds of thousands of persons. Many displaced Bosnian Croats came to Croatia as refugees, and some of these refugees attacked Bosnian Muslim refugees currently living in Croatia. The Croatian government did little to protect Bosnian Muslim refugees from attack. Moreover, the anti-Muslim propaganda regularly heard on the state-controlled television and radio throughout 1993 exacerbated tensions between Muslims and Croats in Croatia.

As of March 1995, the Croatian government was providing refuge to 189,000 refugees from Bosnia and 196,000 persons who have been internally displaced as a result of the war in Croatia in 1991 and thereafter.[92] Officials of the United Nations High Commissioner for Refugees (UNHCR) in Croatia told Human Rights Watch/Helsinki representatives that they estimated that an additional 30,000

---

[92] United Nations High Commissioner for Refugees, Office of the Special Envoy for former Yugoslavia, "Information Notes on Former Yugoslavia," No. 3/95, March 1995. These figures do not include the 97,000 displaced persons and refugees who have sought refuge in the so-called United Nations Protected Areas (UNPAs), most of which remained under Serbian control until mid-1995.

unregistered refugees were living in Croatia in mid-1994. With the notable exception of the forced repatriation of draft-age Bosnian males, UNHCR officials interviewed by Human Rights Watch/Helsinki representatives claimed that the Croatian government's treatment and accommodation of refugees has generally been good. In addition to receiving Bosnian refugees, Croatia continues to accept, and provide aid to, Croats, Hungarians and a very small number of Serbs who have fled or are transported by the U.N. from rebel Serbian-controlled areas of Croatia.

Refugees are required to register with the Social Welfare Center based in the district (opčina) in which they currently reside. Refugees are granted refugee status usually for three months, at which point they must renew their status. According to Maja Kurent, the Liaison Officer for UNHCR at the Croatian government's Office of Displaced Persons and Refugees (ODPR),[93] if a refugee cannot return to his or her home in Bosnia because of continued fighting or fear of persecution, the refugee's status will be renewed. Once the war in Bosnia ends, refugees will be required to return home.

On July 13, 1992, Croatia stated that it could no longer bear the cost of accepting more refugees. However, it said children, the disabled, pregnant women and those with serious medical problems were to be permitted to enter Croatia and were allowed to register as refugees. The admission of other Bosnian Muslim refugees was to be limited to those with assured passage to a third country.[94]

In practice, however, the Croatian government has continued to accept refugees from Bosnia. These refugees are not issued refugee status but are given transit visas, in theory to transit Croatia en route to a third country. However, because the transit visa is valid only for forty-eight hours and foreign governments refuse or delay acceptance of Bosnian refugees, most of the displaced remain in Croatia. Croatia has agreed to accept these additional refugees temporarily, provided that the UNHCR take responsibility for their care and ensure that they are eventually resettled in a third country.

Many refugees have entered Croatia illegally. In February and March 1993, the Croatian government announced that it would grant refugee status to those Bosnians who had not registered as refugees in Croatia. Although many took the opportunity to legalize their stay in the country, many men chose not to register

---

[93] Interviewed by Human Rights Watch/Helsinki representatives on May 31, 1993, in Zagreb, Croatia,

[94] United States Department of State, *Country Reports on Human Rights Practices for 1993*, (Washington, D.C.: U.S. Government Printing Office, February 1994).

with the local authorities because they feared that they would be forcibly repatriated to Bosnia as draft evaders.

In the summers of 1993 and 1994, the Croatian government issued orders that displaced persons and refugees residing in resort hotels along the Dalmatian coast and in Istria be transferred to other accommodations in order to make the hotels available for tourism and to refurbish resort areas. UNHCR confirmed that the Croatian government could rightfully remove the refugees and displaced persons from the hotels, but it asked the government to help provide alternate accommodations. The Croatian government then transferred many of the refugees to collective refugee centers in the village of Gašinci (near Djakovo), to the island of Obonjan (near Šibenik) and other refugee settlements.

In June and July 1994, Muslim refugees refused to leave their refugee accommodations in Istria after the Croatian government ordered that most refugees and displaced persons living in the resort areas of Istria be moved to alternate accommodations. The Croatian government responded to the refugees' refusal to leave the area by refusing to supply them with food. Deprivation of food to the refugees as a way of forcing them to accept a change of accommodations is unnecessarily cruel and potentially harmful for their health and security. Governmental authorities also should not create obstacles that would impede relief efforts of the international relief agencies, such as UNHCR. Although the Croatian government may have a legitimate reason to pursue changes in accommodations, it should try to achieve its objective by means that are less dangerous for the life and health of the refugees.

Although the Croatian government does have an obligation not to discriminate between refugees on account of race, religion or country of origin,[95] some Croatian refugees and displaced persons (i.e., Croats from both Croatia and Bosnia) have been accorded preferential treatment over Muslim refugees. As the conflict between Bosnian Croats and Muslims worsened in 1993, Muslim refugees in Croatia became targets for discrimination and harassment by some local authorities, individual extremists and recently displaced Bosnian Croats. In some cases in 1993, Bosnian Muslim — but not Bosnian Croat — refugees were moved from hotels along the Dalmatian coast, particularly in the Makarska area. According to foreign relief workers interviewed by Human Rights

---

[95] Croatia ratified the Convention Relating to the Status of Refugees in 1992. Article 3 of the Convention states:

> The Contracting States shall apply the provisions of this Convention to refugees without discrimination as to race, religion or country of origin.

Watch/Helsinki,[96] Bosnian Croat refugees also were told that they had to leave the hotels but those who did not leave were allowed to remain. Conversely, local authorities threatened to revoke the refugee status of Bosnian Muslims if they did not agree to leave the hotels. Those refugees transferred to Obonjan island were harassed and robbed by local criminals, and the authorities in Šibenik placed unnecessary restrictions on the refugees' ability to leave the island and travel to the mainland.

Since March 31, 1993, with few exceptions, the police have refused to register Bosnian refugees, especially men of draft age, although some were offered transit visas. Some Bosnian Croats, however, received refugee status. Such an approach discriminates on the basis of ethnicity. Unregistered refugees are not entitled to humanitarian assistance from Croatian government relief agencies and, if arrested, receive an order for deportation to Bosnia.

In other cases, municipal authorities have removed the refugee status of Bosnian Croats and Muslims by categorizing the areas from which they come as "safe." Zenica has been designated as "safe" for Muslims to return and Stolac and Mostar have been designated as "safe" for Croats, and more recently for Muslims, to return. Human Rights Watch/Helsinki believes that although fighting is no longer taking place in some of these areas, inter-ethnic tensions are such that precautions should be taken by the local authorities and agencies belonging to the U.N. or the European Union to ensure the safety of those returning. In particular, Croat-controlled western Mostar and Stolac are still not safe for returning Muslims and, until the local authorities responsible for abuses are removed or correct their abusive behavior, Muslims should not be forced to return to these areas against their will.[97]

FORCED REPATRIATION AND FORCED MOBILIZATION INTO THE BOSNIAN CROAT ARMED FORCES

For a period of time in late 1992 and 1993, the Croatian government refused to grant Bosnian men between the ages of eighteen and sixty refugee status in Croatia, claiming it was complying with a "friendship agreement," signed by the Croatian and Bosnian governments in 1992. The agreement notes that all men

---

[96] Interviewed in Zagreb and Split in August and September 1993.

[97] A forthcoming Human Rights Watch/Helsinki report will examine the status of human rights in the Muslim-Croat federation in Bosnia-Hercegovina.

between the ages of eighteen and sixty have been mobilized for military or work duty in Bosnia, and thus that both the Bosnian and Croatian governments consider Bosnian men who had fled to Croatia as draft evaders, not refugees. As a result, the Croatian government frequently sent Bosnian men back to the battlefront in Bosnia. In 1992, repatriated refugees were left in Croatian-controlled areas of Hercegovina, where they were allowed or induced to join the Bosnian Croat militia, the Croatian Defense Council (Hrvatsko Vijeće Obrane - HVO), or permitted to travel to areas controlled primarily by Muslim and Bosnian government forces.

The repatriation of Bosnian males in 1992 and early 1993 conflicted with the stance then taken by the UNHCR, which considers all Bosnians living outside their country as refugees, irrespective of their age, ethnicity or sex. Because civilians are the targets in the war in Bosnia, the UNHCR argued that those returned to Bosnia would necessarily become vulnerable to abuses of humanitarian law and therefore should not be repatriated.

The Bosnian-Croat "friendship agreement" cannot overrule the obligation of non-refoulement,[98] which is customary international law. The Croatian government, even if it considers the men draft evaders, nevertheless has an obligation to allow them a fair opportunity to claim asylum. The Croatian government cannot decide that all Bosnian men of a certain age are draft evaders and, therefore, force them to repatriate.

The Croatian government repatriated Bosnian men sporadically throughout 1992 and early 1993. After UNHCR and the international community protested such activity, the repatriations stopped for a period and then resumed, only to be protested by the international community again. In some cases, protests from the UNHCR resulted in the return to Croatia of refugees who had been forcibly repatriated to Bosnia.

As fighting between Bosnian Croats and Muslims escalated in late 1992 and in mid- and late 1993, the Croatian government began arresting and forcibly repatriating Bosnians — primarily Muslims, but also Croats and a small number of Serbs — on a wider scale. Unlike in 1992, however, those Muslims being repatriated to Bosnia were not allowed to travel freely or to join the armed forces of their choice. Rather, Croatian government authorities delivered the Bosnian Muslim men to Bosnian Croat officials, who then imprisoned them in abusive jails and detention camps throughout Hercegovina, intending to use them for prisoner exchanges. Others were transferred to the Muslim-controlled area of Mostar, which

---

[98] Article 33 of the Convention on the Status of Refugees. The principle of non-refoulement also is accepted as customary international law and is therefore binding on all states.

had been under siege by Croatian forces for months. Those Bosnian Croats who were repatriated were given HVO uniforms and sent to the front.

The forced repatriation, mobilization or imprisonment of Bosnian male refugees escalated during the summer of 1993, particularly in late July. On July 29, 1993, the field staff of the U.N. Special Rapporteur received reports that Bosnian refugees in Zagreb, Samobor, Split, Pula, Varadžin and the island of Obonjan were being forcibly repatriated to Bosnia.[99] U.N. officials initially were denied access to those arrested.[100] According to the United States government:

> Some 1,500 refugees were arrested in [refugee] camps around ... [Croatia] toward the end of July [1993]. Almost 500 were detained for alleged criminal activity, and 120 were deported to Bosnia-Hercegovina, in contravention of refugee conventions and commitments made by the Government to the UNHCR.[101]

In a case documented by Human Rights Watch/Helsinki, the Croatian police arrested Bosnian men living in Zagreb and detained them in a stadium in the city. Some of those arrested did not have refugee status and were therefore considered to be in the country illegally. Despite their illegal entry into Croatia, the refugees are still protected from refoulement.[102] Others who were arrested and forcibly repatriated had the proper documentation as refugees.

Human Rights Watch/Helsinki representatives also interviewed Muslims and a Bosnian Croat who had been arrested in other parts of Croatia and were then forcibly repatriated to Bosnia. Damir,[103] a Bosnian Croat who was interviewed by

---

[99] U.N. Commission on Human Rights, "Situation of Human Rights in the Territory of the Former Yugoslavia: Fifth periodic report ...," p. 20.

[100] United States Department of State, *Country Reports on Human Rights Practices for 1993* (Washington, DC: U.S. Government Printing Office, February 1994).

[101] *Ibid.* On October 12, 1992, Croatia succeeded to the 1951 Convention Relating to the Status of Refugees and the 1966 Protocol Relating to the Status of Refugees.

[102] Article 31 of the Convention on the Status of Refugees states that contracting parties cannot make adverse distinctions based on illegal entry, as long as the refugees present themselves without delay and show good cause for their illegal entry.

[103] The witness asked that he not be identified and the name used here is a pseudonym. He was interviewed on July 31, 1993, in Zagreb, Croatia.

Human Rights Watch/Helsinki representatives in Zagreb in July 1993, was arrested and forcibly repatriated to Hercegovina just a few days before, but managed to get back to Croatia. He had been arrested by the police in Zagreb after they asked for his identification papers in the street. According to Damir:

> We were headed for my offices [at the magazine where he worked] the day before yesterday [i.e., July 29]. It was about 9:00 in the morning. We stopped in a cafe in Travno [a part of the Novi Zagreb section of Zagreb]. I came in[to the cafe] at about 9:30 a.m.. I saw the police, and they asked me for my documents. I gave them my driver's license, and then they put me in the lorry and took me to the police station. I was held with some people from the refugee camp, mostly Muslims. There were twelve of us: one Croat and eleven Muslims.

Damir and the eleven Muslims were then taken to a sports hall known as Pešćenica, where a large number of refugees had been detained and were being questioned. Damir waited seven or eight hours before being questioned about his entry into Croatia by two men dressed in civilian clothing; minutes of the questioning were taken by a secretary. He was not permitted to call his editor to confirm his account. Damir was then returned to the hall with the other refugees. According to Damir:

> Those who were allowed to stay in Croatia were immediately given a receipt and released. The criteria [for releasing people] was unclear to me. They released a Serb who had arrived from Konjic [in Bosnia] that day, but they didn't release a Muslim [who also had arrived from Konjic that day]. Both of these men have Croatian wives. They let some people come into the hall. A friend of mine came and said he was my lawyer, but they did not let him [see me]. Throughout the day, more people kept coming.

Damir and others were eventually taken to Bosnia by the Croatian police. According to Damir:

> At about 5:00 p.m., they stopped questioning us and called all of us who had been questioned [earlier] to get on a bus. There were about fifty people in one bus. All of us were originally from

Bosnia. Of the men, six were Croats, forty-six or forty-seven were Muslims and one was a Serb. They took us to Tomislavgrad [in Bosnia]. Four women between the ages of twenty-five and twenty-seven also were on the bus. One of them had a refugee card, but her refugee status had expired. Two other women, one of whom had a sixteen-year-old son, also were on the bus but they were older [than the twenty-five year-old and twenty-seven year-old women]. I didn't have any documents with me. The Serb didn't have a refugee card; he had a document saying he had registered with the police. One Muslim from Bosanski Novi had worked in Croatia for fifteen years as a steel worker, but he had been refused citizenship. A woman from Prijedor — her name was either Jasmina or Jasminka — had a refugee card, but I don't know if it was still valid.

We were escorted by the Croatian police [en route to Tomislavgrad]. Every one hundred to 200 kilometers — whenever we crossed into a new municipality — they [i.e., the police] handed over a list of us on the bus to a new police crew, and the new team would [escort us until we got to the next municipality, when another team would assume their role as our escorts]. When we left Zagreb, we were escorted by two police officers on motorcycles and a jeep behind us. When we got to the first change of police, we were escorted by one police car. The Croatian police did not cross over the [Bosnian] border. When we got to the border, a civilian police officer came and took us across [the border]. He called out two or three names and then got off the bus and left us alone. We continued travelling until we got to the military prison in Tomislavgrad [in Bosnia] at about 6:00 a.m..

Damir and the others were held in Tomislavgrad, in a basement which had been partitioned to create three prison cells. Fifteen persons were held in one cell, and the women were not separated from the men. After about thirty minutes, the detainees were taken from the cell, were asked to give their names and were forced to surrender their belongings, including their money. The detainees were taken back to their cells, and a soldier asked the Croats among them to identify themselves. Ten minutes later, the Croats were taken from their cells and were asked how much money had been taken from them earlier. Their money was returned to them. The Croats were then taken back to a cell, where they were held with fifteen Muslims. The Croats and one Serb were taken to SIS[104] to be questioned. According to Damir:

> The man in charge didn't forcibly mobilize anyone into the HVO, but he lectured us about how we had to be loyal and that we should be fighting for our people. The five Croats and the Serb then agreed to join the HVO. I refused.

Damir was allowed to leave the building to buy cigarettes and a copy of the magazine for which he worked to prove his affiliation as a journalist. He was then released and managed to convince a drunk HVO commander to issue a pass which allowed him to re-enter Croatia.

Damir believed that the men who had been pressured to join the HVO were sent to the front lines near Prozor, where Bosnian Croats were battling the primarily Muslim forces of the Bosnian government at the time. Damir did not know the fate of the Muslims who had been in detention with him. Human Rights Watch/Helsinki Watch interviewed scores of Muslims detained in Bosnian Croat prisons in Hercegovina, such as the Rodoč detention center outside of Mostar[105], during the summer of 1993. Many of those interviewed confirmed that they had been brought to Bosnia in a manner similar to what had happened to Damir.

Following vociferous protests by the international community, the foreign diplomatic corps in Zagreb and UNHCR officials, the Croatian government stopped arresting and repatriating Bosnian refugees during the summer of 1993. However, refoulement continued sporadically during the latter part of 1993.

Some local authorities in Croatia have refused to register refugees or to extend the validity of their registration. Police have also conducted checks in refugee encampments to identify and remove those without any papers. In late

---

[104] The Office of Intelligence and Security (Služba Informiranja i Sigurnosti - SIS) refers to the section of the Croatian government responsible for military intelligence. The Bosnian Croat authorities have adopted military structures virtually identical to those in Croatia proper, hence the reference to SIS in Bosnian Croat-controlled areas of Bosnia-Hercegovina.

[105] For accounts describing the treatment of those detained by Bosnian Croat forces as a result of fighting between Bosnian Croat and Bosnian government troops, see Human Rights Watch/Helsinki, "Bosnia-Hercegovina: Abuses by Bosnian Croat and Muslim Forces in Central and Southwestern Bosnia-Hercegovina," (New York: Human Rights Watch, September 1993).

November 1993, the Croatian police visited unregistered refugee encampments in north-central Croatia and compiled a list of draft-age males in the camps. Because the names of the women and children were not taken, the refugees feared that the men would refouled. The Croatian police continue to arrest and detain refugees who have not been granted refugee status. The UNHCR has had sporadic access to the detained refugees.

In December 1993, a group of Bosnian Muslims who had been expelled from Croatia in July and August 1993 and detained in Bosnia by the HVO reportedly were allowed to return to Croatia.[106] However, of those returning, twenty-six were denied transit visas allowing them to enter Croatia and were then denied entry.[107]

In mid- and late 1993, Croats born in Bosnia-Hercegovina but who had been long-time residents of Croatia were being drafted into the armed forces and sent to Bosnia to fight in support of Bosnian Croat forces (HVO). According to the U.N. Special Rapporteur, an unknown number of Croatian citizens were forcibly rounded up by the military on December 15 and 16, 1993, and informed at the Croatian Army barracks that they would be sent to fight in Bosnia.[108] According to the Special Rapporteur:

> there have been reports of intimidation and beatings by the military of those who have refused to comply. It has also been reported that some of those who have refused to comply have had to sign documents under duress indicating that they are "volunteering" to fight in Bosnia.[109]

Since the rapprochement between the Bosnian Croats and the predominantly Muslim forces of the Bosnian government, the situation of Bosnian refugees — both Muslims and Croats — has generally improved in Croatia. However, following the establishment of the Muslim-Croat federation in Bosnia in March 1994, the Croatian government sought to force the return of Bosnian

---

[106] U.N. Commission on Human Rights, "Situation of Human Rights in the Territory of the Former Yugoslavia: Sixth periodic report ...," p. 18.

[107] *Ibid.*

[108] *Ibid.*

[109] *Ibid.*

refugees who came from the federation areas.[110] In September 1994 it announced that it was revoking the refugee status of all such persons but, due to UNHCR intervention, the Croatian government agreed to limit this to persons arriving after September 1994.[111] However, some persons from federation-controlled areas who were registered as refugees in Croatia, prior to September 1994, have been denied renewal of their refugee status, placing them in danger of being refouled.[112] Persons arriving in Croatia from federation-controlled areas after September 9, 1994, no longer qualify for refugee status.

---

[110] United Nations Security Council, Annex to "Human Rights Questions: Human Rights Situations...," p. 27.

[111] *Ibid.*

[112] *Ibid.*

VI. FREEDOM OF EXPRESSION AND THE PRESS

Since assuming power in 1990, the government of Croatian President Franjo Tudjman has taken steps to assume greater control over publicly-owned media and has repeatedly interfered with the independent press, but mostly with the printed rather than broadcast media.[113] Moreover, the government-owned media has at times been used as a vehicle through which President Tudjman's government and the ruling political party, the Croatian Democratic Union (Hrvatska Demokratska Zajednica - HDZ) have exacerbated rather than ameliorated inter-ethnic tensions and hatreds.[114]

Although approximately fifty percent of the media in Croatia is privately owned, the government owns or retains a controlling interest in the primary media sources in Croatia. Other media sources have been "reprivatized" or "restructured" by the government. In the past four years, the Croatian government has consistently used its controlling interest in the media, or cited "economic insolvency," "reprivatization" and "restructuring" as pretexts to force the closure of publications for political reasons. Large-scale layoffs have also been taking place at many government-owned media enterprises, and Human Rights Watch/Helsinki is concerned that fear of losing one's job has resulted in self-censorship by journalists employed at such enterprises.

In addition to direct and indirect government interference in the management and editorial policies of the press, government-owned publishing houses have refused to print, and government-owned distribution companies have refused to distribute, publications critical of the government or the ruling political party, the HDZ.

---

[113] Human Rights Watch/Helsinki has reported on restrictions of press freedoms in two letters to President Franjo Tudjman (February 13, 1992, and May 22, 1992) and in "Threats to Press Freedoms: A Report Prepared for the Free Media Seminar, Conference on Security and Cooperation in Europe," (New York: Human Rights Watch, November 1993). A copy of the May 22, 1992, letter is attached to this report as appendix B. This section includes violations of press freedoms prior to 1992 in order to illustrate the pattern of action taken by the Croatian government to frustrate freedom of expression and the press.

[114] The government-controlled media elsewhere in the former Yugoslavia, particularly in Serbia, but in Bosnia-Hercegovina as well, is also manipulated by the respective governments and warring factions, thus fomenting inter-ethnic animosities and tension.

INTERNATIONAL LEGAL STANDARDS[115]

Freedom of expression is guaranteed by Article 19(2) of the International Covenant on Civil and Political Rights (ICCPR), which Croatia ratified. It states:

Everyone shall have the right to freedom of expression; this right shall include the freedom to seek, receive and impart information and ideas of all kinds, regardless of frontiers, either orally, in writing or in print, in the form of art, or through any media of his [or her] choice.

The only permissible limitations on this right are set forth in article 19(3) of the ICCPR, which permits only those restrictions that:

are provided by law and are necessary:
(a) For respect of the rights or reputations of others;
(b) For the protection of national security or of public order, or of public health or morals.

The term "provided by law" requires more than mere codification of a law. A law must meet fundamental principles of legality, including "knowledge of the existence of the law and accessibility to it by those affected, and sufficient definiteness as to content and meaning."[116]

The European Court of Human Rights has strictly interpreted the second requirement of Article 19(3) that a limitation be "necessary." A "necessary" restriction must meet a "pressing social need;" it is insufficient that its purpose be merely "useful," "reasonable" or "desirable."[117]

---

[115] This section is excerpted and adapted from Helsinki Watch and the Fund for Free Expression, "Poland: Freedom of Expression Threatened by Curbs on Criticism of Government and Religion," (New York: Human Rights Watch, August 1993), pp. 6-8.

[116] Karl Josef Partsch, "Freedom of Conscience and Expression, and Political Freedoms," *The International Bill of Rights: The Covenant on Civil and Political Rights*, p. 220.

[117] *Sunday Times v. United Kingdom*, Judgement of 26 April 1979, Series A No. 30, para. 59.

Moreover, any limitation must clearly be for one of the purposes enumerated in 19(3)(a) and (b). With regard to the purpose of protecting the "rights and reputations of others," the Siracusa Principles state that this limitation "shall not be used to protect the state and its officials from public opinion or criticism."[118] This does not bar a civil cause of action for libel or slander where appropriate, but underscores the principle that a free and open society must tolerate criticism of the government. Similarly, the purposes of security, order, health and morals must be narrowly interpreted to apply to individuals rather than shield the governing institutions from criticism. As the European Court of Human Rights noted in a famous case concerning political defamation,

> [t]he limits of acceptable criticism are accordingly wider as regards a politician as such than as regards a private individual. Unlike the latter, the former inevitably and knowingly lays himself open to close scrutiny of his every word and deed by both journalists and the public at large, and he must consequently display a greater degree of tolerance.[119]

Agreements pursuant to the Helsinki Final Act of 1975 also make clear that laws restricting the exercise of international norms of freedom of expression are inappropriate. At the June 1990 Copenhagen CSCE meeting, participating states agreed on the following:

> No one will be charged with, tried for or convicted of any criminal offense unless the offense is provided for by a law which defines the element of the offense with clarity and precision.[120]

---

[118] Principle 37. The Siracusa Principles were the result of a 1984 meeting in Siracusa, Sicily, Italy of thirty-one legal experts from several countries convened by the United Nations Center for Human Rights and other organizations. The aim of the conference was to examine the limitations and derogation provisions of the ICCPR. See "Symposium: Siracusa Principles on the Limitation and Derogation Provisions in the International Covenant on Civil and Political Rights," *Human Rights Quarterly*, No. 7, February 1985.

[119] *Lingens v. Austria*, Judgement of 8 July 1986, Series A No. 103, para. 42.

[120] Article 5.18, Document of the Copenhagen Meeting of the Conference on the Human Dimension of the CSCE, June 1990.

[E]veryone will have the right to freedom of expression ... The exercise of this right may be subject only to such restrictions as are prescribed by law and are consistent with international standards.[121]

These agreements clearly define both substantive and procedural standards that are unmet by the Croatian government.

CROATIA'S PRESS LAWS AND OTHER REGULATIONS

Croatia's constitution and laws guarantee freedom of expression. The Croatian constitution prohibits and makes punishable calls to incitement to war or resort to national, racial or religious violence.[122] The constitution also allows the country's parliament or president to restrict certain constitutional rights and guarantees during "a state of war or an immediate danger to the independence and unity of the Republic, or in the event of some national disaster."[123]

---

[121] Article 9.1, Document of the Copenhagen Meeting of the Conference on the Human Dimension of the CSCE, June 1990.

[122] Article 16, Constitution of the Republic of Croatia. Also, Article 20 of the ICCPR states that states party to the Convention agree to the prohibition by law of any propaganda for war and any advocacy of national, racial or religious hatred that constitutes discrimination, hostility or violence. The information contained in this section is taken from U.N. Economic and Social Council, Commission on Human Rights, "Situation of human rights in the territory of the former Yugoslavia, Special report on the media..."

[123] Article 16 of the Constitution of the Republic of Croatia states: "Freedoms and rights can be restricted only by law in order to protect the freedoms and rights of other people, the rule of law, public morals and [public] health." Article 17 of the Croatian Constitution states:
> In times of war, immediate danger to the independence and unity of the Republic or during major natural disasters, certain freedoms and laws guarantees by the Constitution can be restricted. [The decision to restrict these rights is made by] the Parliament of the Republic of Croatia, with a two-thirds vote of all representatives, and, if the parliament cannot meet, the president of the Republic [is empowered to make this decision.]
> The scope of the restrictions must be commensurate to the extent of the danger, and cannot have the resultant effect of creating inequality between citizens in regard to their race, the color of their skin, sex, language, religion, or

The April 1992 Law on Public Information introduced high standards for media freedom and established a seven-member oversight body — the Council for the Protection of the Freedom of Public Information — with a mandate to consider private accusations against the press, as well as objections expressed by journalists to actions of public authorities and owners of media enterprises. However, the law on Public Information does not regulate the government-controlled Croatian Radio and Television (Hrvatska Radio i Televizija - HRT), which is regulated under the July 1990 Radio and Television Act. A second oversight council was created for HRT consisting of thirty-five members, fifteen from the parliamentary parties in proportion to their representation in the legislature, ten from HRT and ten from various social institutions. The council's influence is limited and it convenes only rarely, meeting for the first time in July 1994.

The Law on Telecommunications and Post, passed by parliament on June 1994, does not provide political parties or state organs with free access to broadcasting frequencies, apart from the state-controlled television company, Hrvatska Televizija(HTV).[124] Although many state-run media do not provide free, unregulated access to opposition parties, Croatia's Law on Telecommunications and the Post does not guarantee that frequency assignments will not be withheld on political grounds. Although some indepedent broadcasters operate fairly freely in Croatia, others have been denied frequency assignments, apparently for political reasons.[125]

The Law on Telecommunications and Post establishes rules about political propaganda,[126] and obliges the electronic media to report objectively, professionally, impartially and with respect for pluralistic principles.[127] The law

---

national or social origins.

Even in cases of immediate danger for the survival of the state, the rights protected in this Constitution concerning the right to life, prohibitions against torture, [prohibitions against] brutal or degrading treatment or punishment, the legal definition of punishable acts and punishments, [and] the rights to freedom of thought, conscience and religion cannot be restricted.

[124] Articles 55 and 71 of the Law on Telecommunications and Post.

[125] See following section.

[126] Article 63 of the Law on Telecommunications and Post.

[127] Article 57 of the Law on Telecommunications and Post.

provides for the establishment of a Council of Telecommunications, which is in charge of concessions of frequencies and is composed of nine members (four for three-year terms and five for five-year terms). This council was appointed by parliament on October 21, 1994, pursuant to proposals by the government.

Article 64 of the Law on Telecommunication and Post makes Croatian the official language of radio and television, while permitting programs to be broadcast locally in the language of ethnic and national minorities in proportion to the minority's presence in the particular region. The law expressly stipulates that the objective of media outlets should be the promotion of Croatian cultural tradition as well as the promotion of understanding between members of national minorities or ethnic groups.[128]

BROADCAST MEDIA

The main source of information in Croatia is the state-owned and controlled Croatian Television company. Croatian Television (Hrvatska Televizija - HTV) has a monopoly on nationwide broadcasting through its exclusive right to assigned national broadcasting frequencies, as well as a monopoly on the use of government transmitters. This situation is sanctioned by the Law on Telecommunication and Post.[129] The director of HTV is elected by parliament. Croatia's news agency, HINA, is firmly under state control.

Independent broadcast media does exist in Croatia, usually on a local or regional level, and it is generally not obstructed by the government. Five local television stations with varying degrees of independence operate in Zagreb, Split, Rijeka, Osijek, Čakovec and Opuzen.[130] An independent television program commonly referred to as "OTV" (Omladinska Televizija) is broadcast several hours a day and transmits to one-third of the country, primarily in the north. OTV is not broadcast on government-operated Croatian Television. Rather, OTV operates two

---

[128] Article 56 of the Law on Telecommunications and Post.

[129] U.N. Economic and Social Council, Commission on Human Rights, "Situation of human rights in the territory of the former Yugoslavia, Special report on the media ..." For a description of the law, see preceding section.

[130] Committee on Culture and Education, Council of Europe, Parliamentary Assembly, "Information Report on the Situation of the Media in the Former Yugoslavia," January 17, 1994, Doc. 6994, 1403-13/1/94-3-E.

privately-owned transmitters and its broadcasts are not obstructed by the government.

Over fifty local and independent radio stations function throughout the country[131] but their reception is limited to a given region, municipality or locality (e.g., Radio Pag, Radio Ivanić Grad, Radio Zabok, Radio Supetar, Radio Makarska Rivijera). Radio and television broadcasts from rebel Serbian-occupied areas of Croatia and Bosnia-Hercegovina can be heard and seen in areas under Croatian government control. A program called "Slikom na sliku" is shown on state-owned television every evening. The program shows Serbian, Bosnian and foreign television broadcasts of one specific event, thereby allowing the viewer to view several interpretations of the same story. Finally, foreign television broadcasts on CNN, SKY and other foreign satellite channels are readily available to the many households in Croatia that have satellite antennas.

Despite independent and foreign broadcast media sources, the Croatian government sometimes withholds frequencies to programs that are independent of the government or the ruling party. Sixty frequencies are available to Croatia under an international telecommunications agreement but not all have been distributed by the government. Those frequencies and operating licenses that have been allocated usually are given to stations that are sympathetic to the government or ruling party. For example, an Osijek-based television station supportive of the Croatian government and the local HDZ chapter has been given a frequency on which it transmits its programs daily. In contrast, proposals for similar stations in Varaždin and Medjumurje that would have no government or party affiliation have not been granted frequencies.

PRINT MEDIA

Several independent magazines and newspapers generally publish without government interference. *Novi List*, a Rijeka-based daily; *Glas Istre*, a Pula-based regional paper; *Arkzin*, the publication of the Center for Peace, Non-Violence and Human Rights; and the periodical *Erasmus* regularly publish articles critical of the government. In the case of the latter two periodicals, the circulation is small and may not be seen to pose a threat to the government. *Novi List*, increasingly seen as the replacement of the once-independent *Slobodna Dalmacija*, has a circulation of approximately 50,000. It is privately owned and is based in Rijeka, a city governed

---

[131] U.N. Economic and Social Council, Commission on Human Rights, "Situation of human rights in the territory of the former Yugoslavia, Special report on the media ..."

by members of opposition parties, not the ruling HDZ. In 1992, the paper successfully resisted efforts by the government's Agency for Restructuring and Development to appoint a new board of directors headed by a deputy interior minister. The right-of-center weekly *Globus* also publishes articles and interviews critical of the ruling regime generally without interference, as does the Split-based weekly, *Nedjeljna Dalmacija.*[132]

The government holds a virtual monopoly on printing and distribution in Croatia. Vjesnik and Slobodna Dalmacija are the major newspaper publishing houses in Croatia, and both are controlled, directly and indirectly, by the government.The distribution of print media is the monopoly of Tisak, the state-owned chain which controls about two-thirds of the newspaper kiosks in Croatia. The distribution monopoly resulted in the closure of the weekly *Danas* in 1991 and 1992 and, more recently, Tisak refused to distribute a controversial issue of the magazine *Arkzin.*[133]

While taking a number of steps to privatize former state enterprises, including the media, the Croatian government has also used economic pressures to close or obtain control over publications that are critical of the government. In the early 1990's, the Croatian government's Agency for Restructuring and Development oversaw the re-organization of twelve publications published by the government-owned publishing house, Vjesnik.[134] The government agency created

---

[132] "Several predominantly Serbian periodicals are available to the public in Croatia, including the journal of the Serbian Cultural Association 'Prosvjeta,' *Gomirske novine*, which is published partly in the Cyrillic script. There are also journals published in Hungarian and other minority languages." These publications are published independently and not by government-supported institutions. See U.N. Economic and Social Council, Commission on Human Rights, "Situation of human rights in the territory of the former Yugoslavia, Special report on the media..."

[133] U.N. Economic and Social Council, Commission on Human Rights, "Situation of human rights in the territory of the former Yugoslavia, Special report on the media ..."

[134] In 1991, the publishing house Vjesnik published a combined total of eighteen newspapers and magazines, of which only two were reportedly profitable (i.e., the evening daily *Večernji List* and the magazine *Arena*). In addition to the two profitable publications (*Večernji List* and *Arena*), Vjesnik's other publications in 1991, included *Danas, Vjesnik, TOP, Draga, Erotika, Studio*, the former *Start, Svijet, Mila, Astro, Vikend, Auto-klub, Sportske novosti, Sport magazin, Izborov magazin*, and *Video-Studio*. All sixteen publications were experiencing economic difficulties. See "Crne vijesti iz *Vjesnika*," *Nedjeljna Dalmacija*, June 2, 1991, p 14.

a committee which assumed the financial and property-related management for each of Vjesnik's publications. The committee was comprised of four government appointees. Each publication had the right to appoint one person as a consultant to the committee, but that individual would only be consulted about issues directly affecting the representative's respective publication. The committee had the right to replace managing directors but, according to Zdravko Mršić, then director of the Agency for Restructuring and Development, "the content and editorial decisions of the papers would remain in the hands of the current editors."[135] Milovan Šibl, director of the Croatian News Agency HINA and a member of the aforementioned committee, said that the committee "will not interfere with the editorial decisions of the respective publications."[136] Despite such assurances, the government has forced the closure of certain publications that are critical of the Croatian government through economic pressures.

Danas

During both the communist and current regimes, the weekly *Danas* published articles by dissident and opposition groups that criticized the government. However, *Danas* had economic problems and was not a profitable publication of the Vjesnik publishing house. A committee established by the Croatian government's Agency for Restructuring and Development sought to close *Danas*, on the grounds that it was bankrupt. On August 21, 1991, a court rejected the committee's proposal.[137] Although *Danas* was not closed, it was denied access to Vjesnik's printing presses in mid-September 1991, allegedly because *Danas* had not paid its bills.[138] *Danas* then used the printing facilities of the Delo publishing house in Ljubljana, Slovenia. The government then named a new management board (*upravni odbor*) at the weekly in late 1991, and the editorial staff was subsequently changed. A court injunction against the distribution of the paper was issued. When the injunction was declared invalid, the Vjesnik printing firm again

---

[135]"Upad u Vjesnik," *Danas*, June 4, 1991, p. 28-29, and "Crne vijesti iz *Vjesnika*," *Nedjeljna Dalmacija*, June 2, 1991, p. 14.

[136]"Upad u Vjesnik," *Danas*, June 4, 1991, p. 28-29. Šibl was interviewed by Human Rights Watch/Helsinki in Zagreb on May 28, 1991.

[137] Committee to Aid Democratic Dissidents in Yugoslavia, *CADDY Bulletin*, No. 66, August 1991.

[138] "Obavijest Čitateljima," *Danas*, October 1, 1991, p. 6.

refused to print the weekly. In early June 1992, *Danas* ceased publication as a politically independent weekly.

Although *Danas* indeed had financial difficulties for some time, so too had fifteen of Vjesnik's other publications, almost all of which were feature magazines. Human Rights Watch/Helsinki is concerned that *Danas* was among the first of Vjesnik's publications to be targeted for closure by the government because of its independent and critical editorial policy.

Novi Danas

After *Danas* ceased publication in June 1992, Emil Tedeschi, a Croatian emigre businessman resuscitated *Danas* under a new name, *Novi Danas*. The new weekly employed its predecessor's journalists and maintained its independent and critical editorial policy. Because the Vjesnik publishing company refused to print the weekly, *Novi Danas* was printed in Graz, Austria, and Ljubljana, Slovenia. However, when the paper was brought back to Croatia, it was charged a customs duty for being a "foreign publication."

Thereafter, *Novi Danas* was published by the financier's own publishing company, "Emil Tedeschi novine." However, the government-owned distribution company canceled its contract with *Novi Danas* and refused to distribute further issues. According to Tedeschi, the Trgoštampa distribution company, a former Vjesnik sales network, refused to distribute the new weekly, claiming that the distribution contract had been concluded with *Novi Danas*, not with the Tedeschi publishing firm. To ensure that it would not be subject to a financial loss, the Trgoštampa distribution company claimed that the Tedeschi publishing house's financial soundness would have to be established before Trgoštampa would agree to distribute the publication.[139] Trgoštampa then canceled its contract to distribute *Novi Danas* and, due to economic losses, *Novi Danas* ceased publication in September 1992.

While Trgoštampa's business reasons for refusing to distribute *Novi Danas* may or may not be valid, persistent government obstruction of the publication of *Danas* and *Novi Danas* appears to have been politically motivated to silence the publication for its independent or opposition editorial policies.

In December 1992, *Danas* was resuscitated as the publication of the ruling HDZ political party.

---

[139] See Z. Luburović, "*Novi Danas* Thrown Out of Vjesnik Newspaper Stands," *Slobodna Dalmacija*, July 27, 1992, and "Weekly Distributed Despite Repeated Bans," August 18, 1992 as translated in FBIS-EEU.

Slobodna Dalmacija

In the early 1990s, *Slobodna Dalmacija* had a daily circulation of between 90,000 to 100,000 copies. Moreover, the Slobodna Dalmacija publishing house was a profitable firm, with its own printing facilities. Other state-owned Croatian dailies provided news that primarily focused on government activity. In contrast, *Slobodna Dalmacija* printed columns and articles by, and interviews with, left-of-center and other opposition figures and columnists as well as by Croatian government supporters.

In the summer of 1990, *Slobodna Dalmacija* was restructured as a private share-holding company under federal Yugoslav legislation. As a result, all government assistance and involvement ceased. After assuming power, the Croatian government reversed this, contending that the paper had not followed the proper procedure for privatization, thereby allowing the government to make the claim that the paper was still owned, at least in part, by the state. For nearly three years, government officials, members of the HDZ and right-wing opposition groups criticized and tried to discredit *Slobodna Dalmacija*'s editorial policies and some of its journalists as being "too liberal," "communist" or "Yugoslav."

In October 1992, the Croatian government appointed a new board of directors[140] and approximately 70 percent of shares reportedly were sold to state interests, rather than the newspaper's employees, who retained 25 percent of the paper's stock.[141] In March 1993, a new editorial board sympathetic to the government and the ruling party was installed. The paper's journalists went on strike to protest government interference in the paper's editorial policies, but they subsequently returned to work. Soon thereafter, most of the journalists were dismissed or quit. Although *Slobodna Dalmacija* continues to publish a variety of political opinions, it is noticeably more sympathetic to the Croatian government than it was prior to the government's *de facto* take-over of the paper.

---

[140] The members of the new board (*upravni odbor*) were Metod Juršić, the head of the board; Boško Siljeg; Rade Perković, the director of the Croatian National Theatre in Split; and Goran Dodig, the director of the Firule hospital in Split and the Vice-President of the Split-based chapter of the opposition HSLS party.

[141] International Freedom of Expression Exchange, "Croatia: Takeover of Slobodna Dalmacija by the Croatian Government," March 29, 1993, and "Politically Correct *Slobodna Dalmacija*," March 31, 1993.

Feral Tribune

In addition to refusing to print or distribute independent publications, the Croatian government has also levied heavy taxes against publications critical of the government. *Feral Tribune* originally had been a four-page insert published once a week in *Slobodna Dalmacija* when the paper was independent of the government. Three of *Slobodna Dalmacija*'s journalists authored the insert, which satirized persons prominent in Croatian, Serbian and international politics. After the Croatian government obtained a controlling interest in *Slobodna Dalmacija*, *Feral Tribune*'s authors and other journalists from *Slobodna Dalmacija* left the paper and published the insert as a separate publication, adding investigative and critical pieces to the satire.

Feral Tribune was registered as an independent publication in April 1993 with the Croatian government's Ministry of Culture and Education and started publishing on a bi-monthly basis in June 1993. At first, the government-controlled Slobodna Dalmacija and Vjesnik publishing houses in Split and Zagreb, respectively, refused to publish the new magazine. The paper was then printed by the privately-owned Novi List publishing house in Rijeka but is now published in Zagreb. The government-owned distribution companies sell the paper, and it is readily available at most kiosks in Croatia.

On May 3 and June 15, 1993, the paper solicited an exemption from certain taxes, such as the tax on the importation of newsprint, which is granted as a form of public subsidy to the written press in Croatia.[142] *Feral Tribune* did not receive a reply to its requests despite the fact that the legal time limit granted authorities to respond had expired.[143] For this reason, *Feral Tribune* was subject to the same taxes as pornographic publications from which most of the rest of the press is exempt.[144] Its tax payments amounted to one-half of its sales revenue from each issue and the maintenance of such a tax threatened to bankrupt the paper and

---

[142] Reporters Sans Frontieres, as reported by the International Freedom of Expression Exchange, "Croatia: Administrative Measures Against Independent Weekly *Feral Tribune*," September 8, 1993.

[143] *Ibid.*

[144] *Ibid.* Article 19, clause 12, of the Law of Taxation on the Traffic of Goods and Services, exempts most publications from taxes. (See "Zakon o porezu na promet proizvoda i usluge," *Narodne Novine*, br. 36/91, 73/91, 18/92, 25/93, 13/94, 22/94, 28/94 i 48/94.) This law is discussed in greater detail below.

force it out of business. *Feral Tribune*'s editors and journalists appealed their case in court, and the government was forced to repeal the tax.[145]

However, on July 1, 1994, *Feral Tribune* was notified by Croatia's Ministry of Culture and Education that the government's 1993 decision to repeal the tax was being revoked and that the paper would once again be required to pay the aforementioned tax. In its notice, the government acknowledged that *Feral Tribune* was exempt from taxes in the past "because it was properly registered with the Ministry of Culture and Education under number 349 ... as a publication whose topics included satire, politics, economics, culture and sports."[146] Indeed Article 19, clause 12, of the Law of Taxation on the Traffic of Goods and Services,[147] exempts from taxes

> books, brochures, magazines, publications of a professional, academic, artistic, cultural and educational character, school books for pre-school, elementary, secondary and higher education, official announcements, and daily and periodic publications. The republic's organ for education and culture will decide whether a product constitutes any of those mentioned in this clause.[148]

According to the July 1, 1994, notice from the Ministry of Culture and Education, the earlier tax exemption was now being revoked because the publication's "conception and topics had been significantly altered" and it no longer qualified for exemption from taxes under Article 19, clause 12, of the Law of Taxation on the Traffic of Goods and Services. The notice did not state explicitly how the substance of *Feral Tribune* had changed since September 23, 1993, the date the Ministry of Culture and Education had issued its decision to grant *Feral*

---

[145] See Opinion of the Ministry of Culture and Education of the Republic of Croatia dated September 23, 1993. (Mišljenje, Republika Hrvatska, Ministarstvo Kulture i Prosvjete, klasa 612-10/93-01-503, u broj 532-03-1/6-93-01, 23. rujna 1993.)

[146] See "Mišljenje," Republika Hrvatska, Ministarstvo Kulture i Prosvjete, klasa: 612-10/94-01-907, u broj: 532-03-1/5-94-01, Zagreb, 1. srpnja 1994.

[147] See "Zakon o porezu na promet proizvoda i usluge," *Narodne Novine*, br. 36/91, 73/91, 18/92, 25/93, 13/94, 22/94, 28/94 i 48/94.

[148] *Ibid.*

Tribune tax exempt status. Indeed, *Feral Tribune* has generally been a satirical publication since its inception in the 1980s, when the then communist authorities also attempted to quash its criticism of that regime and its leaders. When *Feral Tribune* separated from *Slobodna Dalmacija* and became an independent publication in April 1993, a section dealing with investigative and critical journalism was added to the paper. The paper has not changed its structure, content or critical political position since then. *Feral Tribune* refused to publish an issue in protest of the government's decision but later resumed publication, although its profits were taxed by 50 percent.

Human Rights Watch/Helsinki representatives tried on three occasions in mid-1994 to solicit the views of the Croatian Ministry of Culture and Education concerning its position toward *Feral Tribune* but we did not receive an answer to our queries.

In the midst of international and domestic opposition to the penalization of *Feral Tribune*, the Croatian government announced that Vesna Girardi-Jurkić, the Minister of Culture and Education, was being removed from her post. Shortly thereafter, she was appointed as Croatia's representative to UNESCO. Zlatko Vitez, the new Minister of Culture and Education, requested that the taxation of *Feral Tribune* be abolished, but his request was turned down by the government.[149] Finally, on March 22, 1995, Croatia's Constitutional Court ruled that there were no legal grounds to justify application of the tax on *Feral Tribune* and the Court withdrew the tax. *Feral Tribune* is currently suing the government for redress of financial losses it suffered during the eight months it had to pay the tax.

On December 31, 1993, Viktor Ivančić, the editor-in-chief of *Feral Tribune*, was drafted and inducted into military service and assigned to basic training for several weeks, and then released from military duty. Although Human Rights Watch/Helsinki does not question the Croatian government's right to mobilize persons for military duty, provided they include certain safeguards, we are concerned that Ivančić's conscription may have been politically motivated. To the best of our knowledge, this is the first time an editor-in-chief of a publication has been mobilized into the Croatian Army. Most journalists to whom Human Rights Watch/Helsinki representatives have spoken contend that journalists often are exempt from military service because their work as journalists is deemed to be part of the war effort.

---

[149] Croatian Helsinki Committee, "Notice No. 18," February 8, 1995.

According to the Croatian Ministry of Defense, there is no specific law exempting journalists and news editors from military service.[150] However, in response to our queries, the Croatian Defense Ministry pointed out that, in times of war, those adults who are not active members of the military often are required to perform work duty (*radna obaveza*). Those whose work duty is regarded as important for the state's interests generally are not conscripted into the armed forces. Most journalists and editors employed in the news media are exempt from serving actively in the military because their work qualifies as fulfillment of the work duty (*radna obaveza*) requirement. In order for a journalist to earn exemptions from military duty, however, a journalist's employer (i.e., the newspaper, periodical, television or radio station) must forward a request for the employee's exemption to the Ministry of Defense, claiming he/she is fulfilling work duty. In most cases, the exemption is approved. The Ministry of Defense justified Ivančić's conscription, claiming he had never sent a request for such an exemption.

If, in fact, editors-in-chief are not regularly conscripted, Ivančić's conscription is suspicious. Although Ivančić may have failed to submit a request for exemption to military service, he has long been a well-known journalist in Croatia, and it is highly unlikely that the Croatian Army — particularly in Split — did not know who he was. Although we take no position on the Croatian government's right to draft conscripts — including journalists — we are concerned that Ivančić may have been conscripted into the military because of his paper's opposition stance. Ivančić and his colleagues at *Feral Tribune* have written critically and satirically of the Croatian government, members of the ruling HDZ party, and members of the Croatian military, particularly the military units based in Split. We are concerned that Ivančić's conscription into the Croatian Army may have been used as yet another means to intimidate journalists at *Feral Tribune*.

On July 27, 1995, a group of individuals seized copies of *Feral Tribune* from newstands and then burned them in Split's city center. Right-wing groups praised the vandalism and the Croatian government has reportedly remained silent about the incident. Such violent acts can intimidate news vendors, who may fear to distribute the paper.

Glas Slavonije

A once-independent regional Osijek-based paper, *Glas Slavonije*, was placed under government control on July 25, 1991, precipitating the resignation of the editor-in-chief, Drago Hedl, and the managing director, Vladimir Kokeza. The

---

[150] This information was given to a Human Rights Watch/Helsinki representative, per her requests via telephone, in January 1994.

next day, then commander of the Croatian armed forces in Slavonia, Branimir Glavaš,[151] entered the paper's offices with ten heavily armed Croatian Army soldiers and ordered all those present to leave. Shortly thereafter, Glavaš and other government-appointed members of the paper's executive board appointed new managers at *Glas Slavonije*.

Vjesnik

Vjesnik is the major government-owned daily in Croatia and its editorial policies have generally been supportive of the government and ruling party. However, in 1994, the paper's reporting of the news had been more objective, and it had printed articles critical of the government or ruling party. Possibly in response to *Vjesnik*'s growing independence, its editor-in-chief, Krešimir Fijačko, was dismissed from his post by the government in December 1994.

TRIALS OF JOURNALISTS

Journalists who have written critically about members of the Croatian government have been investigated or charged under the criminal and civil codes. In some instances, when cases went before the courts, the courts generally ruled against government efforts to prosecute journalists for the content of their articles. Despite the somewhat independent efforts of the judiciary, Croatia's government and ruling party continue to harass and intimidate journalists because of the content of their writings, either through arrest, financial pressures, or other modes of intimidation.

Vladimir Šeks, Vice-President of the Croatian government, and Vesna Girardi-Jurkić, Croatia's former Minister of Culture and Education, had proposed that the resoration of a media law from the communist era be considered in Croatia. The proposed law would protect from slander the country's president, the president of the parliament, the prime minister and the president of the constitutional court. Human Rights Watch/Helsinki believes that such a law would criminalize speech against the country's most powerful government officials and would have a chilling effect on the media, effectively barring all criticism of such officials. The proposal has been severely criticized within Croatia, which has diminished the possibility that the bill will be introduced in the parliament. Nevertheless, such recommendations by high-ranking Croatian government officials reinforce the view

---

[151] Glavaš currently is the governor (župan) for the eastern Slavonija, Baranja and western Srijem regions.

that the government is trying to stifle criticism of its policies or of members of the ruling party.

In late May 1992, soon after Šeks was appointed as Croatia's Public Prosecutor,[152] investigatory proceedings were started by prosecutor's offices in Zagreb and Split against *Globus* columnist Tanja Torbarina, then *Danas* columnist Jelena Lovrić, *Globus* editor-in-chief Denis Kuljiš, and the authors of then *Slobodna Dalmacija*'s *Feral Tribune*, namely Viktor Ivančić, Predrag Lucić and Boris Dežulović. The aforementioned persons were accused of violating Article 197 of the Croatian Criminal Code which forbids "spreading false information" and carries a maximum jail term of five years.[153] Some were accused of slander. Charges either were never filed or were dropped in most of these cases, due to lack of evidence and public outcry. However, Jelena Lovrić was indicted and given a suspended six-month sentence for slandering a former government minister she had reported took bribes.

- Viktor Ivančić, Predrag Lucić and Boris Dežulović, authors of *Feral Tribune* (then a supplement of *Slobodna Dalmacija*) faced prosecution for publishing a photo-montage comparing President Tudjman with Stalin and Hitler. Charges were filed in early 1992 but were subsequently dropped in August 1992.

- Denis Kuljiš, the editor-in-chief of the private weekly *Globus*, was charged with "spreading false information" when he published an article on August 16, 1991, advocating cultural and political autonomy for Serbs living in the Krajina region, which was then controlled by rebel Serbian forces.[154] Charges were dropped against him for lack of evidence.

- The district public prosecutor in Zagreb sought to bring charges against Tanja Torbarina, a columnist for *Globus*, "for the criminal act of insulting and slandering the President of the Republic of Croatia, Dr. Franjo

---

[152] Šeks is no longer Croatia's public prosecutor but currently serves as one of four vice-presidents of the Croatian government.

[153] Article 197 of the Croatian Criminal Code was amended by parliament so that it now requires a threat to public order and safety.

[154] PEN American Center, "Serbian and Croatian Independent Voices Under Attack," *Freedom to Write Bulletin*, February/March 1993, p. 2.

Tudjman."[155] This was on the grounds that Torbarina had implied that Tudjman was an illegal squatter in the lavish villa of former Yugoslav President Tito. Specifically, she compared Tudjman's occupancy of the Villa Zagorje to the illegal occupancy of a building by the Croatian Party of Rights (Hrvatska Stranka Prava - HSP), a right-wing political party and opponent of Tudjman's government.[156] The case went to trial and the court ruled in favor of Ms. Torbarina, but the government later appealed the decision to a higher court.[157]

- Jelena Lovrić, a columnist for *Danas*, was taken to court by a government prosecutor and was given a six-month suspended sentence for slandering Zdravko Mršić, the former head of the government's Agency for Restructuring and Development, whom she accused of taking bribes. At the time of Lovrić's article, Mršić was a private citizen and sought redress for slander against Lovrić in a suit separate from the government's court case. Although Mršić, as a private citizen, may have the right to bring a case against Lovrić, Human Rights Watch/Helsinki believes that the government showed an inappropriate interest in a private matter, and did not have direct interest in the suit at the time of its adjudication.

- A Zagreb district court sentenced Croatian journalist Jasna Tkalec to three months in prison for "spreading false information" in an article she wrote for the Karlovac-based daily *Nokat* on June 3, 1991. In the article, Tkalec stated that Serbs were being discriminated against and that their homes were being robbed and destroyed in the city of Zadar.

- Nikola Visković, a professor at Split's Law School and a former member of Croatia's parliament, has been a vociferous critic of the ruling HDZ

---

[155] "Tužba Protiv Tanje Torbarine," HINA story of May 19, 1992, as carried by *Slobodna Dalmacija*, May 20, 1992.

[156] *Ibid.*

[157]In 1992, the weekly *Globus* published an article attacking several prominent female writers in Croatia who are otherwise critics of the Tudjman government. Some of the women sued the paper for slander and libel, but this was a dispute that did not involve the Croatian government; *Globus* is a private paper and the Croatian government was not a party to this case.

party and local and republic governments' tolerance of, or responsibility for, continuing human rights abuses in Croatia. In a November 27, 1992, interview with the Rijeka-based daily *Novi List*, Visković accused Croatian officials — including Croatian Vice President Vladimir Šeks — of committing or condoning human rights violations. Šeks filed suit for defamation — as a private individual — on January 12, 1994.[158] On July 11, 1994, the court ruled in Šeks's favor, but Visković appealed to a higher regional (*županijski*) court.

- In late January 1995, Gojko Šušak, Croatia's Defense Minister, filed a slander suit against Ivan Zvonimir Čičak, Chairman of the Croatian Helsinki Committee for Human Rights, according to Article 7, clauses 1 and 2(m) of the Croatian Criminal Code. Šušak alleged that Čičak slandered him in an interview he gave to the Rijeka-based daily *Novi List* on May 7, 1994, in which Čičak claimed that many in the Croatian Helsinki Committee believed that the Defense Ministry is "a den of organized crime" and that Minister Šušak bore chief responsibility for the conduct of the ministry. At a court hearing in early 1995, Čičak apologized to the court, the legal representative of the Defense Ministry accepted the apology and the case was dismissed.

The judicial decision convicting Visković for defamation and the slander suit brought against Čičak set dangerous precedents permitting trials and convictions of those denouncing human rights violations. Such decisions have a "chilling effect" on others whose public voices are needed to keep governments accountable for their actions or violations of human rights. Also, because Šeks and Šušak are public officials, the court should have followed the *Lingens* precedent[159] and held their cases to a higher standard. If it cannot be shown that Visković or Čičak intentionally published or stated something they knew to be false or that they acted in reckless disregard for the truth, they should not be found guilty of defamation or slander.

---

[158] International Federation of Journalists, citing the Democratic Forum of Rijeka/Fiume, "Action Alert: International Freeedom of Expression Exchange Clearing House," March 4, 1994.

[159] See preceding section concerning international legal standards which describes the European Court of Human Rights's decision in *Lingens v. Austria*.

VII. PARDON AND PROSECUTION OF ALLEGED SERBIAN INSURGENTS

In the past three years, the Croatian government, under pressure from the international community, has amended an amnesty law and adopted a "law of forgiveness," the latter of which is primarily aimed at pardoning persons who joined the Serbian insurgency in Croatia. However, the "law of forgiveness" has been applied inconsistently and trials of insurgent Serbs and others continue, often *in absentia*. Domestic laws regulating crimes against the state have been applied to prosecute thousands of alleged Serb insurgents throughout Croatia. By mid-1994, over 2,200 individuls, mainly Serbs, had been charged with violations of domestic and international humanitarian law and crimes against humanity. While Croatia is to be applauded for its attempts to prosecute accused war criminals, these cases for the most part fall short of internationally accepted standards of fairness and due process. Although Human Rights Watch/Helsinki is not in a postition to determine the guilt or innocence of each defendant, we seek to assure that defendants are given fair trial by an impartial court or jury and that they are afforded all other due process guarantees. While Croatia has taken many steps in this regard, many more are needed to fulfill international guarnatees.[160]

---

[160] The denial of a fair trial and other due process guarantees violates Articles 9 and 14 of the International Covenant on Civil and Political Rights, which guarantee anyone arrested or detained specific rights to due process. Such rights also are guaranteed in Section 13.9 of the CSCE Vienna Concluding Document and Section 5.16 of the CSCE Copenhagen Concluding Document.

The legal analysis contained in this section was initially prepared by Human Rights Watch/Helsinki at the request of the American Bar Association and is contained, in part, in the American Bar Association, Central and East European Law Initiative (CEELI), "Analysis of Croatia's Draft Law on Amnesty," November 19, 1993. See also, Human Rights Watch/Helsinki, "Former Yugoslavia: War Crimes Trials in the Former Yugoslavia," (New York: Human Rights Watch, June 1995).

RELEVANT LEGISLATION

The Amnesty Law: Procedures for Obtaining a Pardon[161]

The language of Croatia's amnesty law was modeled upon a 1977 Yugoslav amnesty law. On November 9, 1990, and December 22, 1992, the 1977 law was revised to reflect the change in regime and to delete any references to the former Socialist Federal Republic of Yugoslavia (SFRJ) and institutions related to that state (e.g., organizations of self-management, references to the death penalty,[162] etc.). The amnesty law was further amended and revised on March 22, 1993.

The 1993 amnesty law sets out the procedures involved in obtaining a pardon, with the decision to grant a pardon residing ultimately with the country's president, with the advice of a court. The court's opinion is delivered to the Ministry of Justice and Public Administration, which then may seek further information from other sources before submitting its evaluation and the petition for a pardon to the president. The law clearly delineates the responsibilities of individual applicants and relevant government bodies and officials. The 1993 amnesty law does not specify who can be pardoned and in which cases pardons can be granted — it is purely procedural in content.

The "Law of Forgiveness"

In addition to the revision of the 1977 law, the Croatian parliament adopted, and President Tudjman signed, a "law of forgiveness" on September 25, 1992.[163] The "law of forgiveness" pardons all those "who committed criminal acts

---

[161] The Croats' use of the words "amnesty" and "forgiveness" in this and the following section may be confusing to some in the context presented here. Although an amnesty law is a criminal law of general applicability that decriminalizes certain conducts for a certain period of time, the Croatian amnesty law described here is a statute that is procedural in nature and that regulates the exercise of executive clemency or presidential pardon. In Croatia, the "law of forgiveness" (described below) is the law which decriminalizes certain acts.

[162] Croatia adopted a new constitution on December 21, 1990, which abolished the death penalty. (See Article 21, clause 2, *Ustav Republike Hrvatske*.)

[163] "Zakon o oprostu od krivičnog progana i postupka za krivična djela počinjena u oružanim sukobima i u ratu protiv Republike Hrvatske," ("Law of Forgiveness from Criminal Prosecution or Proceedings for Crimes Committed in the Course of Armed

during the course of armed conflict in Croatia." The pardon is applicable to crimes committed between August 17, 1990, and September 25, 1992, the date the law went into effect,[164] and was aimed in particular at exempting from criminal prosecution those who joined forces in rebellion against the Croatian government — notably Serbs from the so-called Krajina region and parts of eastern and western Slavonia.[165] In addition to providing an amnesty for those who joined rebel Serbian forces, the "law of forgiveness" also pardons from criminal prosecution persons who committed "crimes *related to* the armed conflict in Croatia."[166]

The "law of forgiveness" was submitted to the Croatian Parliament at the urging of President Tudjman and was hastily passed. It is widely believed that Tudjman was responding to pressure from the international community, particularly the European Community (now the European Union), to extend a conciliatory gesture toward the Serbs so as to better facilitate peace negotiations initiated in London in August 1992.

Conflicts and the War Against the Republic of Croatia"), *Narodne Novine*, No. 58, September 25, 1992, pp. 1305-06.

[164] The law was signed by President Tudjman on September 25, 1992, and was published in the country's legal register *(Narodne Novine)* on the same day. The date of publication in the *Narodne Novine* is the day the law went into effect.

[165] President Tudjman and Croatia's ruling political party, the Croatian Democratic Union (Hrvatska Demokratska Zajednica - HDZ), came to power following multi-party elections in Croatia in April and May 1990. In August 1990, Serbs in the city of Knin rebelled against the new government, which it considered to be nationalist and anti-Serbian. Full-scale war between rebel Serbs and Croatian armed forces broke out after Croatia declared its independence from the former SFRJ on June 25, 1991. Fighting generally ceased by mid-January 1992, when a cease-fire was signed and U.N. troops were deployed primarily in areas that remained under the control of rebel Serbian forces at the time. By early August 1995, Croatian government forces re-captured most of the rebel Serb-held territory in Croatia, although the eastern Slavonia and Baranja regions remain under rebel Serbian contol. During and after the Croatian government's re-capture of the western Slavonia and Krajina areas, the Croatian government stated that "members of Serbian paramilitary units, who [had] been mobilized into such units of their own free will or by force" and who surrendered to Croatian authorities whould be granted amnesty pursuant to Croatian laws. (See "President Tudjman's Message to Croatian Serbs," full text contained in HINA report of August 4, 1995.)

[166] Author's emphasis.

President Tudjman was criticized vociferously by the Croatian public for having acceded to international pressure to adopt an amnesty law for Serbian combatants. The parliament was able to pass the law despite public disagreement because Tudjman's ruling party, the HDZ, maintains a majority in parliament and generally follows the president's wishes.

According to Article 2 of the "law of forgiveness," the state cannot pardon from prosecution those who violated international laws by which the Republic of Croatia is bound. Indeed, international law and domestic Croatian law, which incorporates international humanitarian law, require that crimes against humanity, war crimes and genocide be exempt from any state pardon. Therefore, persons guilty of crimes against humanity, genocide or violations of the 1949 Geneva Conventions and their 1977 Protocols[167] are not eligible for pardon, and members of both Croatian and Serbian armed forces believed to have committed any of these crimes are subject to prosecution for their alleged actions.

Insofar as an individual(s) had been indicted and was being prosecuted for having joined the Serbian insurgency or for having committed "crimes related to the ... conflict" at the time of the law's promulgation, the "law of forgiveness" requires that court proceedings in such cases cease. Furthermore, if someone had already been incarcerated for his/her participation in the rebellion or for the commission of crimes related to the conflict, he/she was to be released from prison. According to press reports, in November 1992 President Tudjman pardoned 104 persons on the basis of the "law of forgiveness."[168] On November 11, 1993, the Croatian Ministry of Justice announced that President Tudjman accepted the recommendation of its Committee for Amnesty and pardoned 133 persons who had been found guilty of crimes against the state. Of the 133 pardoned, eighty-eight were Serbs, forty-one were Croats and four were members of other ethnic groups. Investigations into the cases of an additional 2,516 persons accused of similar crimes were stopped and charges were not brought. Of the 2,516, 1,991 were Serbs, forty-six were Croats, three were Muslims and fifteen were members of other ethnic groups. Of those against whom investigations were stopped, 2,301 were alleged to have been members of Serbian armed forces or paramilitary groups,

---

[167] Croatia became a High Contracting Party to the Geneva Conventions and their Protocols on May 11, 1992.

[168] "Pardons for Serbs, Others Goes Into Effect," FBIS-EEU, November 13, 1992, p. 24, citing November 12, 1992, Agence France Presse report summarizing an article carried in the main Croatian daily, *Novi Vjesnik*, on November 12, 1992.

eighteen were members of the Croatian Army, fourteen were members of the Yugoslav Army (JNA) and 183 were civilians.[169]

As noted, those pardoned included not only Serbs, but also members of the Croatian Army.[170] For example, four members of the Croatian Army were arrested and tried but subsequently set free for the murder of Mr. Damjan Zilić on November 23, 1991, in Zagreb. According to reports received by Human Rights Watch/Helsinki, the four soldiers were tried for the murder before a civilian court in February 1992, but then the presiding judge referred the case to a military court. After two days of deliberation, the military court reportedly asked that psychiatric reports be issued, and the accused were released and remain at liberty. The trial of the four accused soldiers never resumed because they were pardoned under Croatia's "law of forgiveness."[171] The fact that Croatian Army soldiers were included in the pardon remains troublesome, because it allows for the pardon of members of Croatia's own military if they perpetrated gross human rights abuses as crimes defined in Croatia's criminal code, albeit not for war crimes, for which they should otherwise be punished.[172]

Article 3 of the "law of forgiveness" allows the state prosecutor to appeal, within twenty-four hours, the pardon of a person(s) whom the prosecutor believes is guilty of violating international laws. However, a time limit of twenty-four hours within which to appeal a pardon may be too short a period to prepare a proper presentation.

---

[169] Statement of Croatian Ministry of Justice, November 11, 1993. The Croatian government forwarded a copy of the Ministry of Justice's statement to Human Rights Watch/Helsinki. The statement was accompanied by a listing of those pardoned who are identified by name, date of birth, the date of the decision to grant the pardon, the file number of the document granting the pardon, and the criminal code under which the person being pardoned initially was indicted. See also the press release issued by the Mission of Croatia to the United Nations on November 19, 1993.

[170] *Ibid.*

[171] Human Rights Watch/Helsinki asked for confirmation and clarification of these reports concerning the Zilić case from the Croatia government but has never received a reply.

[172] See following section concerning accountability for human rights abuses and criminal activity perpetrated by members of the Croatian Army and police for an explanation of Human Rights Watch/Helsinki's position regarding amnesties for members of a government's own military and police forces.

In practice, if Serbian combatants are pardoned under the "law of forgiveness," it is highly doubtful that these Serbs could return to their homes or places of employment in areas under Croatian government control and not face some type of harassment by former neighbors and colleagues or by members of the Croatian Army or police.

In addition to opposition to the "law of forgiveness" by the Croatian public, Serbs living in Serbian-controlled areas of Croatia view the law as a sham.[173] Indeed, many Serbs point out that the Croatian government continues to prosecute individual Serbs and members of the government of the self-proclaimed "Serbian Republic of Krajina" and its armed forces. Given the continuance of such trials, it is doubtful that members of the Serbian armed forces of these areas will ask for a pardon from the Croatian government in the near future.

Punishment for Subversion and Terrorism

The Croatian government has tried, most frequently *in absentia*, thousands of Serbs accused of "endangering the territorial integrity of Croatia." The Law on Punishable Acts of Subversive and Terrorist Activity Against the State Sovereignty and Territorial Integrity of the Republic of Croatia went into effect on November 4, 1992.[174] This law prescribes between five- and twenty-year prison terms for perpetrators and organizers[175] of the following acts:

a) overthrow of the constitutional and legal system through the secession of regions or places, thereby violating the state's territorial integrity;

b) eviction of citizens and prevention of return of refugees and displaced persons to their homes;

---

[173] This opinion was expressed to Human Rights Watch/Helsinki representatives during our interviews with Serbian authorities in the then Serbian-controlled areas of Knin, Topusko, Okučani and Beli Manastir during the summer of 1993.

[174] "Zakon o Kaznenim Djelima Podrivačke i Terorističke Djelatnosti Protiv Državnog Suvereniteta i Teritorijalne Cjelovitosti Republike Hrvatske," *Narodne Novine*, No. 71, November 4, 1992.

[175] Article 6 of the law specifically states that organizers of the following acts will be treated equally as are perpetrators of such crimes.

c) introduction of a foreign legal, judicial, administrative, monetary, postal or other system associated with the government's authority;

d) prevention of the establishment of the legal order, judicial and executive authority, movement of persons and traffic of goods, health and social welfare, economic or other activity indispensable for the constitutional and legal realization of the rights and duties of Croatia's citizens;

e) endangering the citizenry's peace and security or the state's stability through terrorist acts.

As written, the terrorist law would make possible the prosecution of Serbs who organized the rebellion in August 1990 and those who were part of the self-proclaimed government of the "Serbian Republic of Krajina." The law also might allow for the prosecution of members of the Serbian Democratic Party (Srpska Demokratska Stranka - SDS), the political party that planned, in part, the political and military rebellion of Serbs in the Krajina region.[176] If interpreted broadly, the law would allow for the prosecution of Serbian soldiers who, by virtue of their military affiliation with rebel Serbian forces, obstructed the establishment of Croatian government authority in areas under Serbian control and forced non-Serbs from their homes.

The terrorist law appears not to be used often in proceedings against alleged Serbian insurgents in Croatia. Rather, those accused of crimes against the state are most often charged under Article 231 (formerly codified and also referred to as 236 (b)(1)) of Croatia's criminal code, which makes punishable by a term of at least three years of imprisonment the use of force or "other illegal means" which endangers the territorial integrity of Croatia.[177]

---

[176] Serbian rebels in Croatia and Bosnia-Hercegovina were armed by local SDS officials, by forces of the Yugoslav Army and by paramilitary groups supported by the Republic of Serbia's Interior Ministry.

[177] "Krivični Zakon Republike Hrvatske," (pročišćeni tekst/revised text), *Zbirka Zakona Kaznenog Prava Republike Hrvatske, pročišćeni tekstovi*, (Zagreb: Informator, 1993).

VIOLATIONS OF DUE PROCESS DURING TRIAL AND PRE-TRIAL PROCEEDINGS AND DETENTION[178]

In addition to the civilian judiciary, a military legal system also exists in Croatia. For the purposes of directing military operations during the war in Croatia in 1991, the country was divided into six "operative zones." Likewise, a military prosecutor was appointed and a military court was established in each of the operative zones.[179] The military courts adjudicate cases involving members of the armed forces and civilians charged with offenses related to national security.[180] Although defendants in military courts generally have the same legal rights and privileges as those in civil courts,[181] some procedural differences exist. For example, military courts will accept testimony in the form of written affidavits under circumstances unacceptable in civilian courts. In the first instance of military proceedings, a military prosecutor issues an indictment and the case is adjudicated by a military court. After the military court has rendered its judgment, the defendant has the right to appeal to the Supreme Court of Croatia. Therefore, although a military court adjudicates certain cases in the first instance, a civilian

---

[178] Similar trials of alleged "war criminals," also are taking place in Serbia and Montenegro, in Serbian-controlled areas of Croatia, and in areas controlled by the predominantly Muslim Bosnian government. As in Croatia, these trials do not meet due process standards. The information contained here is a summary of problems associated with such trials in Croatia. For more detailed information regarding such trials, see Human Rights Watch/Helsinki, "War Crimes Trials in the Former Yugoslavia: A Call for Fair Proceedings and Support for the International War Crimes Tribunal," (New York: Human Rights Watch, April 1995).

[179] Letter from Colonel Mirsad Bakšić, State Military Prosecutor, to Croatian Defense Minister Gojko Šušak, February 10, 1993. Listed as number Pov. 2/93 in the Military State Prosecutor's Office in Zagreb.

[180] United States Department of State, *Country Report on Human Rights Practices for 1992*, (Washington, D.C.: U.S. Government Printing Office, February 1993).

[181] Articles 24 to 31 of the Croatian constitution provide due process guarantees for defendants. Article 29, in particular, provides defendants with the right to a fair trial by a competent court, to be present at the trial, to have an attorney and to be informed of the charges brought against him or her.

court (i.e., the Supreme Court) has the power to overturn the decision of the military court.[182]

During the summer of 1993, Human Rights Watch/Helsinki representatives interviewed military and civilian prosecutors in Osijek and Zagreb and asked them to justify the prosecution of alleged Serbian combatants for "armed rebellion against the state" despite the existence of the "law of forgiveness." The responses revealed considerable confusion about "the law of forgiveness." For example, Mr. Pandžić, the military prosecutor responsible for the sixth military zone in Osijek,[183] claimed that the "law of forgiveness" did not apply to Serbian combatants, and that such persons can be tried for "armed rebellion" against the state. According to Pandžić:

> All those who used a gun are guilty of [participating in an] "armed rebellion" [against the state]. The "law of forgiveness" applies only to those who put on a uniform but did not take part in hostilities. Insofar as one participated in the conflict and caused damage to a town, city or village, that person can be prosecuted for "armed insurrection." Even a Serbian soldier who shot at a Croatian soldier during a battle but did not [otherwise] commit a war crime, can be tried for "armed rebellion." The amnesty law does not apply in this case.

When Human Rights Watch/Helsinki representatives asked Stjepan Herceg, then Croatia's Public Prosecutor, the same question, Herceg's reply contradicted Pandžić.[184]

> Those accused of "armed rebellion" are tried in the military courts but all those who have been indicted for this offense can be forgiven. We have not had many recent cases in which a person was indicted for "armed rebellion," and we are to suspend

---

[182] Letter from Colonel Mirsad Bakšić, State Military Prosecutor, to Croatian Defense Minister Gojko Šušak, February 10, 1993 ...

[183] Interviewed by Human Rights Watch/Helsinki representatives on July 15, 1993, in Osijek, Croatia.

[184] Interviewed in Zagreb on July 29, 1993.

the issuing of further indictments for such crimes — you cannot
hold such proceedings any more.

When asked if Serbian troops that participated in the attack against the city
of Vukovar in 1991 could be indicted for "armed rebellion," Herceg replied that
they could not, given the passage of the "law of forgiveness." When told that some
military prosecutors in various municipalities throughout Croatia had a different
view, Herceg replied that he was willing to clear up any confusion among the
military and civilian prosecutors in the country.

In 1992, military courts in seven Croatian cities brought charges against
8,000 persons, most of them *in absentia*.[185] By early February 1993, according to
Croatia's military prosecutor, Croatia's military courts had brought criminal charges
against 29,133 persons, but only a handful were in custody.[186] Most of those
indicted are accused of committing war crimes, illegally using force to alter the
territorial integrity of Croatia, or assisting or actively fighting on behalf of Serbian
and Yugoslav armed forces during the war in Croatia.[187] According to the State
Public Prosecutor's Office, 84.1 percent of those indicted had been charged under
Article 120 of the Croatian Criminal Code, which makes punishable war crimes
against the civilian population.[188] Verdicts had been reached in 42 percent of the
cases brought to court and 14.6 percent of these were appealed to a higher court.[189]
According to the prosecutor's office, 94.6 percent of all such trials are conducted

---

[185] United States Department of State, *Country Report on Human Rights Practices for
1992* ...

[186] Letter from Colonel Mirsad Bakšić,State Military Prosecutor, to Croatian Defense
Minister Gojko Šušak, February 10, 1993 ...

[187] United States Department of State, *Country Report on Human Rights Practices for
1992* ...

[188] See "Osnovni Krivični Zakon Republike Hrvatske," (pročišćeni tekst/revised text),
Zbirka Zakona Kaznenog Prava Republike Hrvatske, pročišćeni tekstovi, (Zagreb:
Informator, 1993), pp. 41-42.

[189] This information was forwarded by Oskar Poje of the State Public Prosecutor's Office
in response to queries by Human Rights Watch/Helsinki in early 1994.

without the presence of the accused and 96.1 percent of those accused are Serbs, 2.2 percent are Croats and 1.6 percent are members of another ethnic group.[190]

In some cases, persons indicted may have been unjustly accused of a crime. For example, a defendant — most often a Serb who was born in, and was a citizen of, Croatia — resigned or was dismissed from his or her job after war broke out and travelled to Serbia. When such a defendant returned to territory controlled by the Croatian government, often to be reunited with family members still living in the area, he or she was arrested by the Croatian authorities and charged with violating the territorial integrity of Croatia or with the commission of war crimes. In such cases, the prosecution often claims that the defendant travelled to Serbia to join the Serbian forces operating in Croatia. The defendant, in contrast, may claim that he or she travelled to Serbia to escape discrimination, to look for employment, or because of fear of being attacked.

Although it is not the role of Human Rights Watch/Helsinki to determine the guilt or innocence of each defendant, we believe that everyone has the right to a fair trial by an impartial court or jury and that they should be accorded all due process guarantees. Unfortunately, persons charged with war crimes or crimes against the state in Croatia often are tried in violation of due process. Many defendants are beaten upon arrest by the military or civilian police. In other instances, the defendant is not allowed to call witnesses to his or her defense. Lastly, when the Croatian government deems that the accused is a combatant, however little evidence points to his or her involvement in armed hostilities, many defendants are tried in military courts.

International humanitarian law distinguishes between international and internal conflicts.[191] If the war in Croatia is deemed to be an international conflict, members of an opposing military force (i.e., those that come from outside the Republic of Croatia) cannot be tried by either civilian or military courts, because they enjoy combatant's privilege.[192] They can only be held as prisoners of war, to

---

[190] *Ibid.*

[191] The Four Geneva Conventions of 1949 and Protocol I govern the conduct of troops in international conflicts. Protocol II and Article 3 common to the Geneva Conventions of 1949 govern the conduct of troops in an internal conflict.

[192] The combatant's privilege is described as a license to "kill or capture enemy troops, destroy military objectives and cause unavoidable civilian casualties." This privilege immunizes members of armed forces or rebels from criminal prosecution by their captors for their violent acts that do not violate the laws of war but would otherwise be crimes under

be exchanged or freed at the end of hostilities. They can, however, be prosecuted for crimes committed before the outbreak of hostilities and also for war crimes, but not for acts of war that do not violate international humanitarian law. If such combatants are prosecuted for war crimes, they can be tried by military courts, provided due process as required by the Third Geneva Convention,[193] is afforded them.

If the war in Croatia is characterized as an internal conflict, combatants can be tried even for the act of taking up arms against the state. Human Rights Watch/Helsinki has consistently held that combatants engaged in an internal conflict should be tried by civilian, not military, courts. They are entitled to all due process guarantees included in the International Covenant on Civil and Political Rights (ICCPR). They should be tried by an independent and impartial adjudicator. By definition, military courts are not independent; they are administrative courts within the executive branch of government. Human Rights Watch/Helsinki believes that military courts should not be used to try civilians under any circumstances. Military courts should have jurisdiction to prosecute a state's own armed forces only for breaches of military discipline.[194] If a state's soldiers commit serious crimes, those military persons also should be tried in civilian courts.

Although the Croatian legal system provides a civilian convicted by a military court the right to appeal to a civilian court, Human Rights Watch/Helsinki believes that civilians should be tried by civilian courts in the first instance. This is particularly important as the court of first instance weighs evidence while the appeals courts rarely exercise a complete review of the defendant's entire case.

Most defendants in Croatia are tried *in absentia*, which violates their right to face accusers and defend themselves, as guaranteed in Article 14(d) of the

---

domestic law. Prisoner of war status depends on and flows from this privilege. See Solf, "The Status of Combatants in Non-International Armed Conflicts Under Domestic Law and Transnational Practice," *American University Law Review* 33 (1953), p.59.

[193] See Articles 84 and 99-108 of the Geneva Convention Relative to the Treatment of Prisoners of War of August 12, 1949, (commonly referred to as the Third Geneva Convention) and Article 75 of the Protocol Additional to the Geneva Conventions of 12 August 1949, and Relating to the Protection of Victims of International Armed Conflicts (commonly referred to as Protocol I).

[194] In a July 1, 1992, letter to Yugoslav military and civilian officials, Human Rights Watch/Helsinki articulated similar concerns about the misuse of military courts and violations of due process during the trials of seven members of the Croatian National Guard in a Belgrade military court on June 26, 1992.

International Covenant on Civil and Political Rights. In interviews with Human Rights Watch/Helsinki representatives, some lawyers and government officials defended *in absentia* trials, but others did not. Stjepan Herceg, then Croatia's Chief Prosecutor, and some local military prosecutors acknowledged that *in absentia* trials are a violation of due process and that, upon capture by the Croatian authorities, the person has the right to be re-tried. According to Mr. Pandžić, the military prosecutor based in Osijek:

> The *in absentia* trials are aimed against soldiers, in most cases. Those who are tried *in absentia* will be re-tried after they are captured. The *in absentia* trials are held for social and psychological reasons, i.e., to supply the victims [of abuse allegedly perpetrated by the accused] with some form of redress or semblance of justice. Insofar as that person [who had been tried *in absentia*] is later captured, a trial must be held again to ensure that he [or she] is granted the right to due process.

Human Rights Watch/Helsinki objects to the use of trials *in absentia* even if a new trial is afforded after capture, because of the likelihood of prejudice in the court that has already reached a decision. If one is to be re-tried at all, the second trial should constitute a whole new trial, not a form of limited review.

VIII. ACCOUNTABILITY FOR HUMAN RIGHTS ABUSES AND CRIMINAL ACTIVITY PERPETRATED BY MEMBERS OF THE CROATIAN ARMY AND POLICE

GENERAL SITUATION

Members of the Croatian military — particularly the military police — have perpetrated human rights abuses and common crimes (such as armed robbery, murder and burglary) with impunity throughout Croatia.[195] This pattern of impunity also prevails in cases in which military forces commit gross human rights abuses in the line of duty. Regular police officers also have been responsible for common crimes that have gone unpunished, but to a lesser extent than members of the Croatian Army.

Human Rights Watch/Helsinki is concerned that Croatian government authorities have allowed individual military police units in various municipalities — particularly in Split — to take the law into their own hands, thereby weakening the rule of law in the country. Having interviewed members of the Croatian Army, police and public in the past three years, Human Rights Watch/Helsinki has found that the civilian police force is afraid of, or prefers not to challenge, the military police in many areas throughout Croatia. On numerous occasions, members of the Croatian police have confirmed that some members of the military police engage in criminal activity and harass or attack refugees and minorities. Despite their acknowledgement of such activity, civilian police officers believe they are powerless to confront the authority of the military police.

Some of Croatia's soldiers are displaced persons who have been "cleansed" from their homes in areas controlled by Serbian forces. Many have lost all their property, members of their families may have been killed or summarily executed and those family members that remain alive often live in shelters or in make-shift or temporary housing. Given their difficulties as displaced persons and their continued service in their country's army, some of these soldiers feel it is their

---

[195] This section deals with accountability for criminal activity by agents of the state within Croatia proper. It does not address violations of the rules of war by Croatian troops in Croatia, by Serbian irregular troops in Serbian-controlled parts of Croatia or by Bosnian Croat forces in Bosnia-Hercegovina. Violations of the Geneva Conventions and other rules of war, and accountability for such crimes, have been and will continue to be documented in other Human Rights Watch/Helsinki reports.

right to confiscate or destroy the property of those who they view as privileged or to blame for their predicament, i.e., Serbs, former members of the Yugoslav Army and those Croats who fled during the height of the war in Croatia but returned to their homes after the fighting had subsided.

It appears that many of the physical attacks against non-Croats were perpetrated by individuals within the ranks of the police or army and were not centrally planned; nevertheless, actions by Croatian government agents are the responsibility of the government, and the government must clearly show that it is trying to curb those actions in good faith. Although the Croatian government has taken steps to dismiss abusive members of the police and army, prosecution of such persons needs to be more vigorously pursued. The following cases illustrate abuses for which members of the Croatian Army and police responsible for such actions have not, to the best of our knowledge, been punished and which are only some of many examples of impunity.

REPRESENTATIVE CASES

Split

In November 1991, Z.L.'s apartment was robbed while he was attending his niece's wedding in Serbia.[196] He immediately returned home and reported the robbery, which appears to have been perpetrated by Croatian Army soldiers. The police instructed Z.L. to return to his apartment and to compile a list of all the items that had been stolen. While Z.L. was in the apartment compiling the list, someone rang the doorbell. Z.L. opened the door to find a soldier ordering him to put his arms up in the air. Z.L. believed that the soldiers were in fact the men who had robbed his apartment, and he slammed the door before the soldiers could enter. The soldiers shot one bullet at the door and Z.L. ran to the window, screaming that he was being robbed and asking that someone call the police.

Soon thereafter, uniformed soldiers and at least two police officers arrived at the scene and they surrounded the building. Z.L. then heard shooting in the hallway. The soldiers who had been at his door broke the lock, came into and shot up the apartment. Z.L. had been hiding on his balcony and when the soldiers broke into the apartment, he jumped over to his neighbor's balcony. While Z.L. was

---

[196] This information is compiled from information examined by Human Rights Watch/Helsinki representatives that included reports from local human rights groups in Split, court documents, petitions submitted by the victim's lawyer and reports in the Croatian press.

jumping to the next balcony the police officer and soldiers outside the building began shooting at him. Z.L. managed to jump over to the neighbor's balcony unharmed but from the street heard a voice on someone's walkie-talkie stating that "the sniper" had been hit and had fallen.

During the shooting, the police officers did not interfere. However, the commander of the second police station arrived with three or four additional police officers and the owner of the apartment on whose balcony Z.L. remained. The owner of the apartment opened the door and entered with the police officers. Z.L. then presented himself to the police, with whom he spent about ten minutes. During that time, the soldiers were yelling at the police to hand Z.L. over, still maintaining they had caught a sniper when, in fact, the soldiers who had initially come to Z.L.'s door had used excessive force without having identified themselves or presented a warrant.

The police refused to hand Z.L. over to the soldiers and, rather, took him to the police station where the police took his statement and then released him. Z.L. then fled Split. He returned in 1993.

In the interim, the Split police sent a criminal report to the Split military prosecutor, asking that an arrest warrant be issued for the break-in at Z.L.'s apartment and for the "attempted murder" of Z.L.. In early 1993, Z.L. went to the prosecutor's office to inquire about the status of the investigation and possible apprehension of the soldiers in question. At the prosecutor's office, Z.L. was advised that it would be best for him to keep quiet and to go home.

On March 25, 1993, Z.L. was served with a notice from the Interior Ministry ordering his expulsion from Croatia.[197] To the best of Human Rights Watch/Helsinki's knowledge, the soldiers who had broken into Z.L.'s apartment and for whose arrest a warrant was issued have not been arrested.

Sisak

The field staff of the U.N. Special Rapporteur have received several reports of the killings of Serbs which the Croatian authorities have failed to investigate or prosecute appropriately. According to one such report, an elderly Serbian woman was murdered and mutilated in her apartment in Sisak on July 30, 1993. Reportedly, the police did not conduct a full investigation and declined to inform the family about the results of the investigation. Neighbors also were afraid

---

[197] For an account of Z.L.'s expulsion, see section concerning citizenship.

to disclose the identity of the perpetrators, especially after the police approached them.[198]

Other Cases

In a November 1994 report, the U.N. Special Rapporteur highlighted some well-known cases of abuse in Croatia that have not been properly prosecuted despite the fact that the perpetrators were arrested and indicted for the crimes, most of which were perpetrated against Serbs. According to the Special Rapporteur:[199]

- In December 1991, Mr. and Ms. Zec and their twelve-year-old daughter were murdered in Zagreb, and several days later, five persons were arrested as alleged perpetrators of the crime. Four of the five suspects reportedly were members of a special police unit. Although the five admitted to having committed the murders, they were released soon after their arrest for procedural reasons and have never been punished. Reportedly, some of the murderers remain in the service of the Croatian Army.

- Milan Krivokuča, the first president of the Independent Railway Union of Croatia, was murdered outside his home in Zagreb on December 17, 1992. The police never completed their investigation, and no criminal proceedings were ever instituted.

- At least nineteen persons were tortured and/or summarily executed and then buried in separate graves in a field south of Pakračka Poljana, probably in late 1991 during the war between Serbian insurgents and the Yugoslav Army and Croatian government forces. Although the Croatian government has cooperated with efforts by a team of international forensic pathologists to exhume the grave and collect forensic evidence,[200]

---

[198] U.N. Commission on Human Rights, "Situation of Human Rights in the Territory of the Former Yugoslavia: Fifth periodic report ...," p. 15.

[199] The following information is taken from the United Nations Security Council Annex to "Human Rights Questions: Human Rights Situations...," p. 23.

[200] See United Nations Security Council, "Letter Dated 24 May 1994 from the Secretary-General to the President of the Security Council," S/1994/674, May 27, 1994, pp. 65-66, for further information concerning the Packračka Poljana exhumation.

those responsible for the crimes have never been held accountable. Some of the reported perpetrators, Croatian forces who had belonged to a special police force, admitted having committed these crimes, but they were all released and criminal proceedings were discontinued.

• The Special Rapporteur received reports concerning eight alleged murders of Serbs in Split in 1992. Of the eight, Gojko Bulović, Nenad Knežević and Dalibor Sardelić were reportedly killed in the "Lora" military barracks. Djordje and Vesna Gasparović, Ivan Nedeljković, Spiro Pokrajac and Magreta Slavić also were murdered. According to the Special Rapporteur, as of November 1994, criminal proceedings had not been instituted in these cases nor had anyone been punished for the crimes.

• The Croatian government still has not held accountable those responsible for the summary execution of Serbs in the town of Gospić in late 1991.[201]

• Croatian Army soldiers responsible for the targetting of fleeing Serbian refugees from western Slavonia and Krajina must be investigated and held accountable. Those responsible for beating or otherwise mistreating Serbs or for the burning, looting and robbing of Serbian-owned property in western Slavonia and Krajina also must be brought to justice for their crimes.

As stated in the preceding section,[202] some Croatian Army soldiers appear to have been pardoned by President Tudjman shortly after the adoption of the "law of forgiveness." Rather than pardon such troops, the Croatian Army must take steps to purge its ranks of abusive soldiers who have committed serious abuses.

In order to keep the military and police subject to the rule of law, Human Rights Watch/Helsinki believes that the Croatian government should prosecute members of its military and police forces for *all* criminal activity — not just human rights abuses and violations of the rules of war — and that such persons should not be subject to a pardon on any grounds. Croatian soldiers or police officers who

---

[201] For an account of these executions, see Helsinki Watch, Letter to Franjo Tudjman, President of the Republic of Croatia, February 21, 1992.

[202] See previous section concerning the pardon and prosecution of alleged Serbian insurgents, particularly information concerning the murder of Damjan Zilić.

have violated domestic criminal law and have been pardoned for their crimes may have been reinstated as members of the Croatian Army or police force. The re-incorporation of such persons into the military or police forces should not be permitted; it encourages such individuals and their colleagues to commit further crimes, including violations of human rights and humanitarian law.

In 1993 and 1994, the Croatian government took some steps to hold accountable those members of the Croatian police force who had committed crimes or violated or failed to protect a person's human rights in their line of duty. The Croatian Interior Ministry has made an effort to purge from its ranks abusive police officers, and the conduct of the Croatian police force had improved since 1992. During a February 1993 meeting with then Croatian Interior Minister Ivan Jarnjak, a Human Rights Watch/Helsinki representative was told that 2,500 persons were being trained as police officers and that instruction in human rights was part of their training. Jarnjak also said the Ministry of Interior was making changes in police personnel throughout the country, citing the Osijek, Gospić, and Podravska Slatina regions as places where personnel changes had taken place and violations committed by the police had decreased as a result. Members of the U.N. peacekeeping mission in Croatia[203] have confirmed that abusive police officers have been dismissed from their jobs and some have faced disciplinary action or prosecution for their misconduct or criminal activity. Despite improvements in police behavior in 1993 and 1994, the civilian police rarely interfered when the military police or soldiers perpetrated abuses in their presence. Police officers deployed in the formerly Serbian-held part of western Slavonia reportedly are professional in their duties, but during the aftermath of the Croatian Army offensive, few dared to confront the military or sought to stop looting or harassment of Serbs by Croatian Army soldiers.

Although the Interior Ministry took some steps to correct abusive behavior of the police, the commission of common crimes and human rights abuses by members of the Croatian Army appears to have worsened in the past three years. The Croatian Defense Ministry has taken few steps to enforce discipline among its troops, particularly the military police. As illustrated in the preceding chapters of this report, military police officers are responsible for many of the violations of civil and political rights in Croatia. Croatian Army soldiers also are responsible for criminal activity and violations of humanitarian law during and immediately after

---

[203] Human Rights Watch/Helsinki has interviewed scores of UNPROFOR and UNHCR personnel throughout the former SFRJ — particularly in Croatia and Bosnia — in the past three years.

the Croatian government's offensives to re-capture the western Slavonia and Krajina regions in May and August 1995, respectively.

The most frequent form of punishment for the commission of crimes or human rights abuses by a Croatian police officer or soldier has been dismissal. Such persons are less frequently prosecuted or imprisoned for their crimes. Although Human Rights Watch/Helsinki welcomes disciplinary action already taken by the Croatian authorities against abusive military and police officers, we believe that the Croatian government should more vigorously prosecute and punish police officers and soldiers guilty of criminal activity, including human rights abuses. Such steps would work to strengthen the rule of law in Croatia.

GOVERNMENT INFORMATION

In mid-1993, Human Rights Watch/Helsinki requested information regarding Croatian government efforts to hold accountable members of the Croatian Army and police for their crimes; we requested this information from the Croatian Ministries of Defense and Interior, respectively, and the Office of the Public Prosecutor. The Defense Ministry and the State Military Prosecutor's Office forwarded our request to the Public Prosecutor, who retains oversight of military court proceedings. The Public Prosecutor's Office and the Interior Ministry responded to our reports on numerous occasions.

In response to our request, the Interior Ministry provided an overview of reports of the commission of crimes in Croatia perpetrated by members of the Croatian police from January 1, 1992, to July 31, 1993.[204] Although the overview provides government statistics regarding the commission of crimes by the Croatian police, Human Rights Watch has not obtained equally detailed information concerning the prosecution of such police officers and their eventual conviction for their crimes. Statistics refer to cases in which arrest warrants were issued or criminal charges filed against accused police officers and the cases were forwarded to the state prosecutor, who then was to bring the case to trial.

According to the Interior Ministry's overview, from January 1, 1992, to July 31, 1993, (a nineteen-month period) members of the police were charged with

---

[204] Human Rights Watch/Helsinki translated the document into English. A copy is attached as Appendix D of this report. The report was entitled, "The Croatian Interior Ministry's Overview of the Commission of Crimes in Croatia from January 1, 1992, to July 31, 1993, Including Those Perpetrated by Members of the Croatian Police." The data contained in this and the following paragraph are taken from this document.

committing thirty-four murders and ten attempted murders, twenty-one cases of larceny and sixty-six cases of grand larceny, twelve cases of robbery and seventeen cases of fraud. Police officers were also charged with having "endangered life and property through generally dangerous acts or devices" (a charge which usually pertains to the unlawful use or display of weapons) in sixty-nine cases, illegally appropriated public property in fourteen cases, seriously harmed the physical integrity of a person in thirty-five instances, participated in a fight in twelve cases, and abused their official position in fifty-two cases. Police officers were also charged with the following crimes in less than ten instances: manslaughter, threatening public safety, seriously endangering public safety, rape, attempted rape, violent behavior, illegal possession of firearms and explosives, and terrorism.

According to the State Military Prosecutor, as of early February 1993, criminal proceedings were initiated against 1,469 Croatian Army soldiers in the third operative zone, i.e., the area in and around Zagreb.[205] The largest number of these proceedings (578 or 40 percent) were initiated against soldiers accused of committing criminal acts against the property of Croatian citizens.[206]

According to the Croatian government, as of early 1993, members of the Croatian Army were arrested, tried and/or imprisoned for violent crimes outside the area of conflict in the following instances:[207]

- In 1992, sixty-five members of the Croatian Army were indicted for murder and seven for attempted murder in the city of Osijek. All the cases

---

[205] Letter from Colonel Mirsad Bakšić, State Military Prosecutor, to Croatian Defense Minister Gojko Šušak, February 10, 1993. Listed as number Pov. 2/93 in the Military State Prosecutor's Office in Zagreb.

[206] *Ibid.* Two hundred sixty-eight (i.e., 18 percent) of the criminal proceedings were initiated against soldiers accused of endangering the safety of persons and property; 234 soldiers (or 16 percent) were indicted for "violating the public and legal order;" 224 (or 15 percent) of the proceedings were instituted against soldiers accused of endangering the safety of public traffic. Another 118 criminal proceedings (or 8 percent) were initiated against soldiers for acts "endangering the life and bodily safety of persons;" the majority of these charges concerned attacks on fellow Croatian Army soldiers.

[207] The following information is taken from a letter sent by Vladimir Šeks, then Croatia's Deputy Prime Minister, to Amnesty International. The letter was in response to Amnesty International's queries and was published by the Information Department of the Croatian Ministry of Foreign Affairs in "Newsletter 12," April 29, 1993, pp. 9-13.

were brought to court and, as of early 1993, fourteen verdicts had been handed down.[208] Forty-four of the victims were Croats, twenty-two were Serbs and three were Muslims.

- In the areas of Dalmatia within the jurisdiction of the Split military prosecutor, fifty-five persons were charged with murder and attempted murder. All of the accused were members of the Croatian Army when the crimes were perpetrated. Of those indicted, fifty-one were Croats, two were Muslims, one was a Serb and one a Slovak.[209] Of the eighteen persons who were killed as a result of the crimes, fourteen were Croats, three were Serbs and one was a Muslim.

---

[208] Mr. Šeks's letter does not state whether the verdicts proclaimed the innocence or guilt of the defendants.

[209] Again, Mr. Šeks's letter does not indicate whether the accused were brought to trial or the verdicts of the court.

IX. HUMAN RIGHTS MONITORING IN CROATIA

The Croatian government has been cooperative with international human rights organizations. The prosecutor for the international tribunal established by the U.N. to adjudicate war crimes and crimes against humanity in the former Yugoslavia, the Special Rapporteur for the U.N. Commission on Human Rights for the former Yugoslavia and international forensic experts have acknowledged the assistance and cooperation of the Croatian government. The Croatian government also has consistently cooperated with and provided information to Human Rights Watch/Helsinki. However, following the re-assertion of Croatian government authority in the Krajina area in August 1995, access to some areas was restricted to international and domestic monitors.

Despite its generally positive stance toward international human rights monitoring efforts, members of the Croatian government, the ruling political party and segments of the government-owned media have sought to demonize and discredit the work of members of local human rights groups. The concept of a "non-governmental organization" is relatively new and generally not well-understood in Croatia. Non-governmental organizations did not exist openly during the communist era and some segments of society and the government equate "non-governmental" civic activity as "anti-governmental" or "anti-Croatian." Criticism by high-ranking government officials can be inflammatory and may have contributed to attacks by individuals on human rights workers and their property in Croatia. On October 31, 1994, the home of Slobodan Budak, a lawyer and member of the Croatian Helsinki Committee for Human Rights, was vandalized in the town of Karlobag. The police classified the case as a burglary and reported that Alen Vignjević, a twenty-one-year-old policeman, had confessed to the crime. However, the Gospić district attorney declined to bring a criminal prosecution, and Vignjević was released after his confession.[210] In other cases, human rights advocates such as Nikola Visković were sued for libel, slander or defamation by Croatian government officials.[211] Some human rights advocates in Croatia have

---

[210] Letter to Croatian President Franjo Tudjman by the International Helsinki Federation (Vienna), December 5, 1994.

[211] See preceding section concerning freeedom of expression and the press, trials of journalists and others.

been threatened or harassed by private individuals and, in some cases, by government agents because of their human rights activity.

It is the responsibility of the government and its agents to uphold the law, prevent violence and promote respect for the civil liberties of all — irrespective of one's ethnic, religious, political or other affiliations. Unfortunately, members of the Croatian government have sought to discredit the work of local human rights activists rather than to work with them to improve civil and political rights in Croatia. Vladimir Šeks, one of Croatia's vice-presidents and deputy speaker in parliament, is arguably the most vocal critic of human rights advocates in Croatia. Ironically, Mr. Šeks is a former human rights advocate who was imprisoned by the former communist regime for the expression of his civil and political rights.[212] While Mr. Šeks has a right to his own opinions, he also has a duty, as a public official, to ensure that the rule of law is respected in Croatia. Human Rights Watch/Helsinki is concerned that inflammatory criticism of human rights workers by Mr. Šeks and other members of the government and the state-controlled press may incite violence against such activists and may impede their ability to work.

---

[212] A 1982 Helsinki Watch publication, now out of print, addressed Mr. Šek's case and the persecution of fellow dissidents in the former Yugoslavia. (See Helsinki Watch: "Freedom to Conform," August 1, 1982.)

X. CONCLUSIONS

The most abusive elements of the Croatian government are the institutions responsible to the Ministry of Defense. In some cases, soldiers who commit abuses are displaced persons who have lost everything in the war in Croatia and believe that, as victims of the war and defenders of the country, they are above the law. Other soldiers, too, appear free to act with impunity. In other instances, the military police in an area have taken the law into their own hands, and refuse to respect the ruling of the courts or the civilian authorities.

Members of the Croatian government and ruling HDZ party are divided on the issue of human rights: a moderate wing is highly critical of the Ministry of Defense and continuing human rights abuses while members of a more conservative wing defend the ministry and continue to be apologists for violence and crimes committed or tolerated by the government forces. President Franjo Tudjman has not publicly demanded that his ministers — particularly Defense Minister Gojko Šušak — take steps to prevent and punish human rights abuses perpetrated by government agents. Although President Tudjman regularly proclaims his support for the rule of law and respect for civil and political rights, he has not been steadfast in ensuring that those rights are respected in Croatia.

Although the Croatian government has incorporated into domestic law the tenets set forth in international human rights documents, government policies do not always respect those guarantees. Moreover, ambiguity in the laws is exploited in ways that infringe on the rights guaranteed in international agreements to which Croatia is a party and in domestic Croatian law.

Conservative members of the ruling HDZ party, President Tudjman and some members of his government are intolerant of a free press which is critical of the country's leaders and their policies. Croatia's independent printed press has been consistently harassed and intimidated by government officials, and the government has forced a change in editorial policies or the closure of some independent media. While the Croatian government has taken some steps to improve its human rights record in other areas, it has systematically tried to curb freedom of the independent press in Croatia.

In 1993 and 1994, violence against Serbs in Croatia declined, and the most serious problem facing the Serbs and other minorities in Croatia at that time was the denial of citizenship to some non-Croats and those not born in Croatia. Although the government has taken steps to correct the arbitrary denial of citizenship to residents of Croatia, the government refuses to accept the proposition that non-Croats who were residents of Croatia at the time of its independence be granted citizenship. Moreover, following the reassertion of Croatian government control in the formerly rebel Serbian-held areas of western Slavonia, Lika, Banija, Kordun and the Dalmatian hinterland in May and August 1995, harassment of and violence against Serbs, destruction of property owned by Serbs, and the burning of formerly Serb-populated villages has been documented or reported. Nevertheless, the Croatian government allowed such abuses to continue with impunity during the first weeks following the Croatian Army's victory.

Although Croatia's legal and judicial community generally has strived to develop and maintain its independence and impartiality, the court system is still not free of ethnic bias and political manipulation. Many still do not trust the court system and do not bring their grievances before government institutions designed to remedy abuses. However, in cases where the aggrieved have taken their cases to court or branches of the government, such persons often have received rulings in their favor or have been accorded some form of redress. Croatia's constitutional court has generally adhered to professional standards, despite government pressure to politicize the judiciary. However, some local military and conservative civilian officials have refused to abide by the law and disregard rulings of the courts with which they do not agree.

In general, refugees have been treated well by the Croatian government but efforts in 1993 and early 1994 to forcibly repatriate Bosnian males was a serious violation of refugee rights in Croatia. Many of Croatia's human rights problems are directly or indirectly related to the hundreds of thousands of refugees and displaced persons who have sought refuge in Croatia. Forcible evictions, discrimination and mistreatment of minority groups and other violations might decrease if better efforts were made to accommodate refugees and displaced persons. While the Croatian government must abide by its obligations under the 1951 Convention Relating to the Status of Refugees and its 1961 Protocol, the international community must accept more refugees and be willing to aid those displaced persons and refugees who continue to seek refuge in Croatia.

XI. RECOMMENDATIONS

TO THE GOVERNMENT OF THE REPUBLIC OF CROATIA

Human Rights Watch/Helsinki calls upon the Croatian government to abide by its obligations under the International Covenant on Civil and Political Rights (ICCPR). As a member of the Organization on Security and Cooperation in Europe (OSCE), Croatia also has a responsibility to abide by the Helsinki Final Act and subsequent OSCE documents (including Conferences on the Human Dimension held in Copenhagen (1990), Paris (1990), Cracow (1991) and Geneva (1991)) and other international and regional human rights instruments.

In an effort to correct violations of civil and political rights in areas of Croatia which remain under government control, Human Rights Watch/Helsinki offers the following recommendations:

General Recommendations

- Hold accountable members of the Croatian Army and military police who commit human rights abuses and common crimes. Gojko Šušak, Croatia's Defense Minister, and Mate Laušić, chief of the military police, should be held responsible for ensuring that discipline is enforced and maintained within the ranks of the Croatian Army and military police. In particular, the Defense Ministry must make clear to the military police and members of the Croatian Army that they do not have jurisdiction over civilians.

- Cease all efforts by government or political parties to compromise the independence of the judiciary and take measures to strenghten its independence. Ensure respect for the rule of law and the judgement of the courts. The practice of some military officials who ignore the decisions of Croatia's courts and other civilian bodies must cease. Croatian President Franjo Tudjman must make clear that the military is not above the law.

- The Croatian government should take steps to ameliorate inter-ethnic tensions and hatreds in Croatia, specifically in areas over which the Croatian government has recently reasserted control. Local and regional authorities should be required to do likewise. In this respect, the activities of local human rights groups should be supported and their recommendations should be considered by the government. Also, the state-controlled media should refrain from misrepresenting facts because such misrepresentation often breeds resentment of and misunderstanding among Croatia's various ethnic groups.

- In October 1992, a law was passed allowing for the establishment of an ombudsman,[213] who was appointed by President Tudjman. The ombudsman is supposed to be independent of the government and act after all other remedies have been exhausted. However, the ombudsman's activities and authority are limited; frequently the ombudsman's activity is constrained to writing letters of recommendation on behalf of the complainant.[214] The ombudsman's office should be strengthened in the following ways:

> a) The authority of the ombudsman to investigate grievances should be expanded. Insofar as the ombudsman has reason to believe that the complainant was not afforded due process at some point, the ombudsman should be able to examine the response of governmental bodies from which the complainant has not obtained redress.
>
> b) the ombudsman should work closely with domestic non-governmental human rights groups.
>
> c) The ombudsman should be assured easy access to high-ranking members of the government, to whom he or she can bring grievances and concerns of complainants, if necessary.
>
> d) The ombudsman should be appointed by a multi-ethnic, non-partisan body, possibly a parliamentary committee comprised of members of various national and ethnic groups and political parties. In order to ensure independence from the government, the head of state should not appoint the ombudsman.

---

[213] See relevant legislation in *Narodne Novine*, No. 60, October 1, 1992, pp. 1336-38.

[214] U.N. Commission on Human Rights, "Situation of Human Rights in the Territory of the Former Yugoslavia: Sixth periodic report ...," p. 15.

e) The statute creating the position of ombudsman should be amended to give the ombudsman authority to investigate, to obtain documents from state agencies, to obtain access to facilities, to file complaints with agencies, and to initiate judicial actions (both remedial, on behalf of victims, and criminal, against perpetrators of human rights abuses), without prejudice to the powers of prosecutors and courts.

Citizenship

- Distinguish newly arrived immigrants from persons who resided in Croatia at the time it declared its independence from the former SFRJ. The norms set out in the current citizenship law can reasonably be applied to those citizenship applicants who have never resided in the former SFRJ or were never citizens of that state. However, more liberal criteria should be adopted for and applied to citizenship applicants who lived in Croatia and considered it their primary community while it was still part of the former SRFJ.

- Regulate the status of permanent residence for aliens, with clearly spelled out rights and obligations, in conformity with international standards.

- Issue work permits and honor past commitments to disburse pensions, welfare and medical benefits to all those who had been employed in the republic prior to Croatia's declaration of independence and who currently continue to work in Croatia without citizenship.

- Make known to the applicant the specific reason for his or her denial of citizenship.

- Provide a right of appeal by establishing an impartial, non-partisan and multi-ethnic review commission to review the cases of those denied citizenship.

- Avoid arbitrary deprivation or denial of citizenship and work actively to minimize statelessness in Croatia.

Treatment of Serbs and Other Minorities

●   Take steps to investigate, prosecute and punish those responsible for the deliberate targeting or killing of civilians during the western Slavonia and Krajina offensives, and the looting, burning and destruction of Serbian villages or property following the offensives.

●   Revise, and possibly repeal, the decree on the Temporary Expropriation and Control Over Certain Property so that it does not collectively punish Serbs who remained in "enemy" territory in recent years.

●   Reinstate all those unlawfully dismissed from their jobs because of ethnic or political affiliation.

●   Establish a provisional court of human rights, as provided for in Croatia's Constitutional Law on Human Rights and Freedoms and Rights of National and Ethnic Communities or Minorities in the Republic of Croatia. The law establishes a provisional court of human rights, which would serve as a precursor to the eventual establishment of a permanent court of human rights in Croatia.[215] The provisional court should be established and its composition should be multi-ethnic. The court must be apolitical, impartial and independent. However, in early 1995, the U.N. Special Rapporteur reported he had been informed that the court would not be created if Croatia's request for admission to the Council of Europe was accepted. The Special Rapporteur is concerned that if the court is not established, individuals who were victims of human rights prior to Croatia's accession to the Council and, by extension to the European Convention on Human Rights, would not have adequate legal remedies.[216]

---

[215] U.N. Commission on Human Rights, "Situation of Human Rights in the Territory of the Former Yugoslavia: Sixth periodic report...," p. 15. The text of the constitutional law is contained *Narodne Novine*, No. 34/92, June 17, 1992, p. 832.

[216] U.N. Economic and Social Council, Commission on Human Rights, "Situation of human rights in the territory of the former Yugoslavia: Tenth periodic report ...," p. 13.

Evictions from State-Owned Housing

- Immediately cease all evictions of persons who were the lawful tenants at the time of Croatian indepedence from apartments formerly owned by the JNA or SSNO, otherwise known as "military apartments."

- Facilitate the return of those who have been forcibly evicted from their homes to return without fear of reprisals or harassment.

- Return property illegally confiscated and provide compensation to owners for property damaged during a forcible eviction.

- Hold accountable all those who used unlawful threats of violence against persons being evicted from their homes or against persons observing the eviction.

- In light of their repeated violations of the law and abuse of their official position, revoke the power of local military housing commissions to evict persons from their homes. Those powers should devolve to a civilian administrative body and ultimately to courts with judicial review over the agency's decisions.

- Respect Croatian law regulating and the independent decisions of the Croatian judiciary concerning evictions, housing and the temporary use of apartments. Insofar as laws, decrees or multi-lateral and bi-lateral agreements regulating the use of "military apartments" conflict, a professional, impartial commission should be formed to resolve the inconsistencies in the relevant laws, decrees and agreements. The commission also should revise any laws and regulations whose ambiguity has been or could be manipulated to justify forcible evictions. Under all circumstances, due process and the right to appeal should be accorded to all parties facing eviction. The recommendations of the commission should be considered by the Croatian parliament and codified into law.

- Explore avenues through which to ensure adequate long-term housing for refugees and displaced persons — including soldiers. Adequate housing for the displaced and refugee population will lead to a decrease in forcible evictions and in the violence that often accompanies such evictions. The housing and settlement of displaced persons and refugees should be aided by the international community.

Treatment of Refugees

- Allow Serbs displaced as a result of the Croatian Army offensives in western Slavonia to return to their homes without fear of retribution.

- Grant refugee status without discriminating on the basis of the refugee's ethnic identity.

- Cease all obstructions of the deliverance of humanitarian aid to Muslim civilians loyal to Fikret Abdić.

- Cease and refrain from the forcible repatriation of Bosnian refugees and permit the return those refouled in the past.

- Cease all discriminatory practices based on ethnic affiliation associated with the settlement and registration of refugees.

- Encourage tolerance of and respect for refugees among the local population and take steps to prevent the marginalization of refugees and displaced persons from the general population.

- Increase police patrols in areas where violence against refugees and minorities — and their property — has taken place or is likely to occur.

Freedom of the Press

- Allow journalists to report freely without fear of reprisal. Journalists and others should not be dismissed from their jobs or prosecuted for their writings or the expression of their opinions, no matter how unpopular with the government, ruling party or general public.

- Revise existing Croatian legislation allowing public officials (including members of the government, parliament and the ruling HDZ party) to bring libel, slander and defamation suits and criminal charges against journalists and others critical of public figures or the government or its policies to conform with international standards.

- Cease all efforts to force the closure or compromise the editorial policies of various media forms in Croatia.

Protecting the Right to Due Process

- Investigate and punish police and military officers responsible for treating persons in detention in a cruel, inhuman or degrading manner, or for the practice of torture.

- Accord due process to all persons accused of crimes, whether or not in detention, including those accused of "violating the territorial integrity of Croatia" or other acts defined as "terrorist" activities or war crimes.

- Provide all detainees with immediate and regular access to attorneys. Members of the Croatian legal community and the government are working to revise Croatia's code of criminal procedure to allow access to a lawyer upon arrest. Such efforts should be welcomed and encouraged by the government.

- Grant the accused the right to be present at trial as well as the right to remain silent and not to be compelled to testify against oneself.

- Provide compensation for unlawful arrest or detention.

Ensuring Accountability for Human Rights Abuses and Crimes Perpetrated by Members of the Croatian Army and Police

- Prosecute military and police personnel guilty of committing human rights abuses or other crimes, particularly those responsible for such crimes during or after the Croatian Army's re-capture of the western Slavonia and Krajina regions. Although the Croatian government has dismissed members of the Croatian Army and police for criminal behavior, those guilty of such crimes generally are not prosecuted and imprisoned for their crimes.

- The Croatian authorities should also increase efforts to initiate or complete investigations of military and police personnel accused of committing war crimes during the 1991-92 war with rebel Serbian forces in Croatia. Although the Croatian government claims to be investigating violations of international humanitarian law by its forces, few persons have been arrested and brought to trial for such crimes. In particular, those guilty of the 1991 summary executions of Serbs in the areas of Gospić and Pakračka Poljana should be brought to justice.

Human Rights Monitoring

• Work with domestic human rights activists in Croatia with a view to strengthening the rule of law and increasing respect for civil and political rights in Croatia. Halt public attacks on human rights monitors by public officials.

• Continue to cooperate with international human rights monitoring missions and the international war crimes tribunal.

TO THE UNITED STATES AND MEMBERS OF THE EUROPEAN UNION

The influx of refugees and displaced persons into or within Croatia has led, either directly or indirectly, to the commission of many human rights abuses in recent years. At a minimum, the international community must be willing to accept refugees and displaced persons and provide assistance to those who have sought protection in Croatia. Such action could help prevent further human rights abuses in Croatia. In particular, the construction of housing for displaced persons and refugees would help alleviate some of the violations connected with forcible evictions.

Germany and the United States, in particular, have great influence with the Croatian authorities. Both states have publicly and vociferously condemned human rights abuses perpetrated by Bosnian Croat forces and have publicly criticized the government of the Republic of Croatia for aiding such abusive forces politically, economically and militarily.[217] Both Germany and the United States have been successful in pressuring the Croatian government to use its influence with the Bosnian Croat forces in order to correct the abusive behavior of the latter in Bosnia-Hercegovina. Germany and the United States should use their influence

---

[217] The U.S. government also has been particularly critical of continued "ethnic cleansing" by rebel Serbian forces in Croatia.

with the Croatian government to effect similar improvements in civil and political rights in Croatia proper and to ensure that those responsible for abuses during or following the 1995 Croatian Army offensive in western Slavonia and in the Krajina region are brought to justice. Such pressure should be exerted both publicly and privately.

The United States generally has employed "private diplomacy" with the Croatian government and has effected some positive results utilizing such avenues. However, Human Rights Watch/Helsinki believes that public criticism of continuing human rights practices in Croatia would help bolster the democratic forces within the ruling party, the government and the public which are opposed to continuing government practices that violate human rights. Such public criticism would force President Tudjman to correct the abusive behavior of some government agencies on the national, regional and local levels. Also, the U.S. and German governments' public support for the improvement of civil and political rights in Croatia, in concert with the European Union, would help bolster those within the ruling party, human rights groups and other organizations and institutions which are working to effect respect for the rule of law and human rights in Croatia.

APPENDIX A: RESPONSE FROM THE CROATIAN GOVERNMENT TO HELSINKI WATCH'S FEBRUARY 1992 LETTER

REPUBLIC OF CROATIA
MINISTRY OF FOREIGN AFFAIRS

41 000 ZAGREB, Visoka ulica 22
Phone: 041/443-012 – Fax: 041/427-594

Zagreb, March 13th, 1992.

Helsinki Watch
New York

Dear Sirs,

We would like to inform you about the standpoints of the Government of the Republic of Croatia on observation of human rights concerning the letter of U.S. Helsinki Watch Committee dated February 13th, 1992.

With kindest regards,

Deputy Minister
Božidar Gagro

STANDPOINTS OF THE GOVERNMENT OF THE REPUBLIC OF CROATIA ON OBSERVATION OF HUMAN RIGHTS AS THE RESPONSE TO THE LETTER OF THE U.S. HELSINKI WATCH COMMITTEE DATED FEBRUARY 13, 1992

I.

The Government of the Republic of Croatia has consistently taken efforts for a peaceful political solution of conflicts on the territory of the Republic of Croatia along with maximum engagement of the world community, for an agreement reached in negotiations on all issues concerning the co-existence among the members of all nations, who are at the same time citizens of the Republic of Croatia.

The war, which the Republic of Croatia did not wish and which it wanted to avoid, has led to huge sufferings of the population, destruction and damages of the property as well as the occupation of a part of the territory of the Republic of Croatia.

The first victims that were killed in Croatia were Croats, members of the Croatian police forces at the Plitvice and in Borovo Selo. After these incidents the killings of the civilians of Croatian nationality commenced; this was followed by the massacres in Croatian towns and villages (Dalj, Erdut, Struga, Pecki, and others); the crimes over the civilian population reached its culmination during the air attacks and heavy artillery attacks hitting hospitals, churches, houses, and other civilian targets.

This resulted in 3,169 dead and about 12,000 missing[1] persons as well as 17,254 wounded persons. Some whole regions in the Republic of Croatia have been destroyed, while the respective population of Croatian and other non-Serbian nationalities have been liquidated, expelled or situated into concentration camps.

The number of the captured persons located in about 40 concentration camps under Serbian control is supposed to be in the range of 8,530, but the precise data are not available because the access to a great number of camps is not possible. According to our knowledge so far, 72 % of the captured who are in the concentration camps are civilians, which is contrary not only to basic human rights but also to the regulations of martial law.

About 720,000 persons have been expelled and they have taken refuge away from their homes; among them there are 374,000 who have been accommodated in Croatia. The greatest part of the displaced Serbian population had been in fact evacuated by the Serbian authorities before the attack of the so-called JNA and other Serbian forces on the areas in question took place, so that the remaining population could be destroyed without fear that people of Serbian nationality could perish too.

---

[1]The number of the dead persons stated here refers to those cases which were identified according to strict world-accepted criteria. All the others have been carried as missing persons although a major part of them is dead.

Complete destruction has hit 18 hospitals and medical centers, while 14 facilities have been destroyed by half[2]. The damages on the cultural heritage of the Republic of Croatia are incalculable and beyond estimability: 470 cultural monuments have been destroyed or damaged, whereof 241 are churches or monasteries. Furthermore, 181 historical sites plus 63 other properties of cultural interest, such as museums, libraries, etc., have been destroyed or damaged.

A number of towns have been completely or partially destroyed (Vukovar, Osijek, Dubrovnik, Gospi, ibenik, Dalj, Erdut, Vinkovci, etc.), while many Croatian villages on the temporarily occupied territories have been burnt down and then levelled with the ground, including cemeteries (elije, Kijevo, Pecki, villages in Konavli region and in the hinterland of ibenik and Zadar as well as in Lika, etc.). There are 35,800 completely destroyed flats/apartments, and 174,200 apartments destroyed to a greater or smaller extent, which makes the total amount of damages, along with the damages on the community infrastructure, be in the range of US $ 4.5 billion.

About 30 % of economic facilities have been destroyed, and the direct damages ascertained so far are estimated to be in the range of US $ 19 billion. More than 25 % of arable land in Croatia have been involved in war operations where harvesting of autumn produces and sowing was impossible. About 148,000 heads of cattle have been killed. About 145,000 people do not work because they were expelled or because their enterprises and factories have been destroyed. Ecological damages due to the bombardment of the oil refinery in Sisak, activities of the enemy which damaged the environment in the Plitvice Lakes area, and in the river of Cetina, where oil was discharged from hydro-electric power plant and whose dam is still mined; further environmental damages can be easily perceived in forests that have been felled down relentlessly while the timber has been taken away out of Croatia. The damages on the plowfields where bombs and missiles are scattered all around are beyond any estimability.

In every war there is a lot of destruction of the national wealth. In this war, however, this is not a matter of incidental war destructions but this is the case of intentional destroying of everything that can remind of autochthonous population that is, according to the same plan, foredoomed to rub-out, too.

Beside the so-called JNA, citizens of Serbia, and Serbs from Bosnia and Herzegovina and Montenegro who took part in the aggression on Croatia, Serbia organized, which is also confessed by the President of Serbia, an armed rebellion of a part of Serbian population in Croatia. At the beginning, this rebellion was oriented against legitimate and legal institutions and representatives of the Croatian authorities (including the representatives of Serbian nationality who did not agree with violence). But in the course of time, in accordance with the plan of the organizer, the rebellion developed into a showdown in a form of an armed conflict with non-Serbian population, primarily Croats.

Unfortunately, in this war in which military formations of the Republic of Serbia including the so-called JNA, do not observe one single basic wartime regulation, it is difficult to have full control over the behaviour of all members of the Croatian Army and

---

[2]The data originate from January 10, 1992.

Police forces. It is also necessary to point out that owing to a great number of expellees (displaced persons) an efficient and continuous control over their behaviour is impossible, so this also renders individual criminal activities possible, either in civilian clothing or having the visual identity of the Croatian Army.

The Croatian Government is aware that some crimes have been committed also by persons wearing the uniforms of the Croatian forces, because these persons have been arrested and prosecuted, and part of these crimes has been depicted in Croatian press. The Croatian Government insists that such individuals, without any difference with regard to those coming from the enemy side, be deprived of freedom and that pre-trial investigation and trial proceedings be instituted against them, because they cast a serious stain upon the democratic system of the Republic of Croatia. On several of its sessions, the Government required reports from the competent departments on violations of human rights and required that, in spite of objective difficulties concerning the ascertainment of the perpetrator, investigation and other legal procedures be accelerated, in order that such cases are clarified and that those who are responsible for them are punished. The special stress is on their greater commitment to prevent the recurrence of similar cases.

The Government of the Republic of Croatia wants to point out in particular, that none of these abuses had been committed by the order of any body of Croatian authority nor has it in any way been approved, justified or hushed up. It is a matter of instances of outrageous behaviour of some individuals which unfortunately occur in any war. Despite the fact that Croatia has found itself in a position where it must canalize all its forces to defend the country, the Government of the Republic of Croatia, despite of all the difficulties it faces along the way, carries on a constant control over the functioning of the executive power in accordance with the Constitution of the Republic of Croatia, its laws and principles of the international law, there where the institutions of the state of Croatia can reach. Unfortunately, the legal system has been suspended on the occupied areas of the Republic of Croatia, which make one quarter of its territory, and this area is inaccessible for the legal bodies of Croatian authority. Therefore, bodies of Croatian authority cannot be held responsible for human rights violations on these areas.

The demand for internationalization in solving the problem of the war against Croatia originated just from the Government of the Republic of Croatia. In this sense it was required that the Monitoring Mission of the European Community be sent with the aim to prevent further violations of human rights and to protect the non-Serbian population exposed to terror and genocide by the so-called JNA and other Serbian formations as well as terrorists from a part of Serbian population in Croatia.

The Government of the Republic of Croatia has several times sent an invitation to international organizations that investigate observations of human rights to visit Croatia, to gather the data and inform the world public about the truth with regard to the war of Croatia. This is why we express our thanks to the Helsinki Watch Committee for the attention it has dedicated to the events in Croatia and for the attempt to present the facts about abuses in an objective manner. We repeat our invitation to the Helsinki Watch Committee to tour the occupied areas in Croatia, concentration camps in Serbia and on the temporarily occupied parts of Croatia, and to inform the world public about the matter-of-fact conditions of human rights.

The Minister of the Interior of the Republic of Croatia, Mr. Ivan Vekić, is ready to present the facts concerning the work of his Ministry to the Congress of the United States of America.

The principle of law-abidance and equality of all citizens before the law make the basis on which Croatia builds its democracy and intends to come back to the family of European countries. Since the beginning of war conflicts on the ground of Croatia, the Government was almost on each of its sessions discussing information on various forms of violations of law and also of the violations of human rights. Several commissions have been founded with the aim to examine the crimes committed or to investigate the indicia which might refer to the crimes; also were established the Commission for Treating Persons Captured in Armed Conflicts in the Republic of Croatia as well as the Commission for Search of the Missing Persons. The Office for Inter-ethnic Relations was founded with the purpose to care for the rights of national minorities and of ethnic communities; the Office for displaced persons (expellees and refugees) was founded, and its task is to take care about accommodation and aid to persons who had to leave their homes in order to avoid death. These bodies have been cooperating with the corresponding international bodies, offices and non-governmental organizations that deal with these problems (International Red Cross, Caritas, United Nations Commissioner for Refugees, UNICEF, and others).

Clear standpoints concerning observance of human rights and consistent use of law regulations have been set out in a series of statements and communications from the sessions of the Government of the Republic of Croatia. The principles carried on by the Croatian Government are founded on international standards referring to protection of human rights, of rights of national and ethnic minorities, and on the international law of war in cases where these regulations are applicable.

The democratic legal system has been established in the Republic of Croatia by means of the Constitution of the Republic of Croatia, laws and regulations being founded on it, where the Constitutional Law on Human Rights and Liberties and on Rights of Ethnic and National Communities or Minorities in the Republic of Croatia takes up a special place. Please note that, in compliance with the Constitution, there is no death penalty in Croatia.

On November 22, 1991 the Government of the Republic of Croatia requested from the United Nations, European Community, Conference on European Security and Cooperation as well as from the governments of the members of these organizations to undertake all possible that lies within their capacities with the view to establish a standing international court for war crimes and for other crimes against humanity and international law. The Government of the Republic of Croatia points out in its request that in spite of indisputable competence of court and judicial authorities of the Republic of Croatia concerning these crimes, foundation of such a court of law would mean an efficient aid to its population exposed to the "Greater Serbian" aggression accompanied by barbarian destructions and instances of the violence not recorded in the recent history of Europe. At the same time this would be of great importance for the international community too, because it would warn all perpetrators of war crimes that they will not remain unpunished, no matter whether they have committed the crimes themselves or they have committed them by following the orders they are obliged to refuse to obey.

ıne competent departments of the Government of the Republic of Croatia are ready to make available to the international court all the necessary documents and to enable a free insight into all relevant facts.

The basic principle governing the relations between nations and states is the principle that conflicts are to be solved in a peaceful way. The endeavors of the Government of the Republic of Croatia to avoid a war conflict can be seen from the letters addressed to the Government of the Republic of Serbia (the first such letter was sent on February 22, 1991) and to the former federal bodies.

We will cite extracts from some minute records taken on the sessions of the Government of the Republic of Croatia, which express our commitment to a peaceful solving of all controversial issues, to strict observance of human rights and of rights of national minorities and ethnic communities as well as to observance of lawfulness in the operations of the state bodies.

1.   On the basis of the decision passed on its session on May 14, 1991, the Government of the Republic of Croatia sent a note of protest to the Government of the Republic of Serbia, in which it reads, inter alia:

"Relying on the foundations of the Constitution of the Republic of Croatia it is a firm decision of the Croatian Govrnement to continuously initiate, develop and assure full respecting of rights and freedoms of all citizens, irrespectively of nationality, creed, language or cultural heritage. There is not one single controversial issue in connection with life and status of a citizen, including issues connected with national affiliation of the citizens of the Republic of Croatia, which cannot be solved thorough legal procedures within the existent institutions of the legal system of the Republic of Croatia.

The Govrnement of the Republic of Croatia has announced to the United Nations and important international organizations, that any group of experts or politicians who wish to convince themselves in observation of human rights and civil liberties by the governmental bodies of authority are welcome at any time and on any part of the Republic.

In spite of the strategic guidelines set forth and of international norms, the Republic of Croatia has been for a long time facing a flagrant, constant and systematic interference of the Republic of Serbia in interior affairs of the Republic of Croatia, for which the Government of the Republic of Croatia possesses pieces of incontestable evidence.

In the statements and actions of the representatives of the public authority of the Republic of Serbia at first a tacit support and now also an open support has been given to the Chetnik and other extremists.

There are verified data on illegal supply of weapons, ammunition, equipment and food from the territory of the Republic of Serbia to terrorist groups operating in the Republic of Croatia.

Once again we want to point out that there is really no need for any protection by the Republic of Serbia to the citizens of Serbian nationality in Croatia. All civil rights and political liberties as well as a cultural autonomy are warranted to them by the Constitution of the Republic of Croatia. A great majority of the Serbs in Croatia supports the legal authorities of the Republic of Croatia, and they disassociate themselves with embitterment from defecting and violent activities of extremist and Chetnik groups and individuals who pull down foundations of coexistence between Croats and Serbs and who initiate deep distrust, intolerance and, what is the most dangerous, hate.

Many Serbian politicians stayed in Croatia without referring to legal bodies of authority. Every visit of theirs meant initiation of new instances of intolerance and a new wave of outlaw violence, and it annulled the efforts of Croatian authorities to make a political solution of the problems evolved in the coexistence between Croats and Serbs in Croatia possible by way of negotiations. Instigating appearances and addresses of a member of the Government of the Republic of Serbia, Minister for Links with Serbs outside the Republic of Serbia, Stanko Cvijan, and Milan Paroški provoked even tragic events in Borovo Selo, just at the time when the condition in that area was somewhat stabilized and when some real possibilities for a peaceful solution were present.

The leaders of the Serbian Renewal Movement and of the Serbian Radical Party proclaimed publicly that their members and units pitched into from the Republic of Serbia (Vojvodina) were active participants, and they assumed responsibility for the crimes committed. Instead of taking legal steps against the criminals, the bodies of authority of the Republic of Serbia have remained mute or, even in the high state bodies, they attempt to justify the crimes by adducing the need that the allegedly endangered Serbian population in Croatia be protected in this way, while they try to present massacres as a deceit stemming from the Croatian authorities.

It is significant that the aforementioned minister for Serbs outside Serbia recognizes the terrorist focus in Croatia as a "legal institution", and that he cooperates with this focus and offers it open support. At the same time he turns a deaf ear to the invitation sent to him by the representative of the Government of the Republic of Croatia on February 22, 1991, that they meet and in an open-minded and direct conversation discuss and jointly propose a solution of open issues.

On account of all this the Government of the Republic of Croatia is addressing a sharp protest to the Government of the Republic of Serbia and urges vigorously from the Government of the Republic of Serbia that in the future it does not allow organizing of actions directed against the Republic of Croatia on its territory, and that it arrests and prosecutes the criminals who participated in cruel killings of Croatian policemen. At the same time we suggest that in direct negotiations between the members of the Government of the Republic of Croatia and of the Government of the Republic of Serbia or their parliamentary delegations we come to solutions which will serve well to a peaceful disentanglement of Yugoslav crisis."

2.   In connection with serious incidents that took place in Ilok and its surroundings on July 8 and 9, 1991, the Government of the Republic of Croatia addressed the following protest to the Presidency of SFRY on July 10, 1991:

"The Government of the Republic of Croatia addresses a severe protest to the Presidency of SFRY on account of serious incidents in Ilok and its surroundings on July 8 and 9, 1991.   On the first day, members of JNA destroyed a car belonging to the Ministry of the Interior of the Republic of Croatia by fire from an armoured car, and they killed one and wounded three Croatian policemen. The following day, on July 9, 1991, during an attack by an army aircraft on a Croatian National Guard base near Ilok one member of the Guard was killed by machine-gun bursts and two were badly wounded.

The Government of the Republic of Croatia demands that the attacks of the members of JNA on the police forces of the Republic of Croatia be discontinued immediately, that JNA stops carrying on all aggressive activities on the ground of Croatia, and that JNA units pull back into barracks, in accordance with Brioni Agreement.

The Government of the Republic of Croatia demands that the incidents in Ilok and its surroundings be examined by a mixed expert commission who will ascertain the facts."

3.   On July 26, 1991, the Government of the Republic of Croatia addressed a severe protest to the Presidency of SFRY, Federal Executive Council and Federal Secretariat for National Defense, which reads as follows:

"In the night of July 25, 1991, members of JNA opened artillery and tank fire from the territory of the Republic of Serbia, near Bogojevo, onto the places of Erdut and Bogojevci in the Republic of Croatia.   Several tens of large-calibre shells hit public facilities and caused great destructions and human losses. So far nine killed members of the Ministry of the Interior of the Republic of Croatia have been found in the ruins, while seventeen were wounded. After the attack from Vojvodina had ended, obviously in a synchronized manner, JNA units showered mortar shells from the village of Bijelo Brdo, too, targeting at a group of members of the Ministry of Interior of the Republic of Croatia in Erdut. The JNA unit used 120 mm calibre mortars.

All the attempts to help the wounded and to transport the dead were hindered by the the commander of the Garrison in Osijek. Moreover, he gave a bestial command to shoot at ambulances, which was executed. This savage attack of JNA on lives and property of citizens and police forces of the Republic of Croatia is only the last in a string of similar ones which - along with terrorist barbarian acts assisted by JNA - have marked all the more stronger aggression on Croatia. (...)

The Government of the Republic of Croatia is addressing to the Presidency of SFRY, Federal Executive Council and Federal Secretariat for National Defense a severe protest against brutal attacks of Yugoslav Army on the territory of the

Republic of Croatia, against all the more open aggression in which numerous lives of Croatian citizens have already been lost.

The Government of the Republic of Croatia requires an urgent and thorough investigation on all these cases and urges that the perpetrators are brought to justice, that any use of arms by JNA against the population and police forces of the Republic of Croatia is thwarted, that Yugoslav army on the ground of Croatia pulls back to barracks in compliance with the Brioni Declaration as well as that the responsibility be ascertained for all those in the military hierarchy who are superiors to the local commanders whose units committed war crimes. If these requirements are not fulfilled, we will consider JNA to be beyond control of the federal institutions, and we will further consider it to be an army of occupation whose only aim is destruction of life within Croatian population, occupation of Croatian territory and removal of legal Croatian authorities from power."

4.   On the same occasion the Government of the Republic of Croatia sent a notification to the Government of the Republic of Serbia, where, beside the description of the event, also the following comment is made:

"The Government of the Republic of Serbia is responsible for this aggressive, brutal and barbarian act, because it was committed on its territory against persons and facilities on the territory of the Republic of Croatia. The Government of the Republic of Serbia has done nothing to prevent the attacks from its territory and to subdue assaults involving bloodshed by terrorists on the Croatian ground. It has not been detecting crimes nor has it been punishing them. Since all the appeals we have sent to you for the purpose of putting an end to terrorism and of resolving all controversial issues exclusively by peaceful means have remained without any effect, we want to assure you, that the Government of the Republic of Croatia will take all the appropriate measures in order to protect its population and its territory."

5.   On August 19, 1991, the Government of the Republic of Croatia condemned with embitterment a criminal terrorist attack on the rooms of the Jewish Community in Zagreb and on the collective tomb on Zagreb cemetery Mirogoj, and it demanded from the investigating officials their maximum involvement in disclosing this criminal act.

6.   At the session held on September 24, 1991, the information on the death of Mr. Ante Paradžik, Vice President of the Croatian Party of Rights, was discussed and the Ministry of the Interior and the Ministry of Justice and Administration commissioned to take measures for the acceleration of the investigation on this event and to inform the Government about the results as soon as possible, and the Ministry of Information was instructed to inform the public that the Government had expressed its sympathy with regard to this deplorable incident.

7.   At the session held on October 13, 1991, Mr. Franjo Gregurić, President of the Government, informed the Government about the arrest of the member of the Government Mr. Muhamed Zulić, who, as a civil person who also enjoys immunity of a

member of the Government of the Republic of Croatia, is in the military prison in Banja Luka, and about the steps that had been taken for his release.

8.   At the session held on October 16, 1991, the Government condemned most severely the deportation of 12,000 citizens of Ilok, Bapska, Šarengrad and other neighbouring places, which referred to inhabitants of Croatian, Czech and Slovak nationalities. Special resolution on this was passed at the session held on October 19, 1991, and a protest was sent to the Monitoring Mission of the European Community; international organizations and institutions were notified, too.   Unfortunately, neither international institutions and organizations concerned with protection of human rights nor the United Nations, or, as far as we know, the Helsinki Watch have reacted.

9.   At the session held on October 19,1991, the Government condemned severely the occurrences of forming irregular armed groups and gangs under the political influence of some political parties and their self-willed activities.   The Government also put the Ministry of the Interior under obligation to take vigorous repressive measures, within its competencies, against any violation of valid regulations by irregular armed groups and gangs which threatens public law and order and functioning of legal bodies of authority.

10.   At the session held on November 22, 1991, Mr. Ivan Vekić, Minister of the Interior, rendered oral information to the Government about the circumstances and reasons for arresting Mr. Dobroslav Paraga and Mr. Milan Vuković. After having been arrested they were given over to the investigating legal authorities who would, on the basis of the investigation results, make a decision on possible continuation of the trial proceedings.

11.   At the session held on November 29, 1991, the Government of the Republic of Croatia charged the Ministry of Defense to make a report on the procedures of the military police and the military investigation bodies against colonel Mile Dedaković and about the circumstances and facts which had led to the injuries of the person during the investigation procedure, which will be based on the statements of the operatives, medical report and the evidence of the prisoner in custody. It was concluded that the Government of the Republic of Croatia, after it has evaluated the reports, should take a stand and propose measures within the competencies of state bodies, while the Ministry of Information should make the public acquainted with the conclusion of the Government of the Republic of Croatia.

12.   On February 4, 1992, the President of the Republic convened a session of the Government with the topics "Current Condition and Problems of Functioning of the Constitutional State". The session was attended also by the Head of the Office for Inter-ethnic Relations of the Government of the Republic of Croatia, Mr. Milan Đukić. For the purpose of strengthening institutions of the democratic political system and institutions of a constitutional state, the Government of the Republic of Croatia concluded, inter alia:

1.   The Government of the Republic of Croatia condemns any threatening of democratic political institutions and each violation of principles of a constitutional state, and especially violations of basic rights and liberties of a man and a citizen, irrespectively of his national, religious or any other affiliation.

2.   The Government of the Republic of Croatia will, via competent ministries and offices, additionally monitor and analyze current states and conditions as well as problems in order to make impossible any activity aimed at weakening of democratic institutions of the political system and of institutions of a constitutional state.

3.   The competent ministries are bound to make agencies from their scope of work and its employees acquainted with the purpose, contents and way of application for each new regulation, and in this sense to strengthen the control of a municipal administrative bodies and organizations which exert public authorizations. In particular they must assure equal treatment and application of rules. All ministries, and especially the Ministry of Justice and Administration, Ministry of Defense and Ministry of the Interior, are obliged to inform the Government of the Republic of Croatia immediately of any violation of the legality principle they get any knowledge of.

4.   The Office for Inter-ethnic Relations of the Government of the Republic of Croatia will keep on monitoring the implementation of liberties and rights by members of minority communities, and will be instructing persons whose rights or liberties have been infringed to commence appropriate legal proceedings before the competent legal, administrative or other authorities.

5.   The Decree on interior affairs during the state of war or imminent danger for independence and integrity of the Republic of Croatia must be applied with utter restriction while the activities taken on the strength of this Decree must be immediately reported to the Ministry of the Interior or the Ministry of Defense (depending on the agency which undertook these activities) as well as to the competent pursuing bodies. The Ministry of the Interior or the Ministry of Defense will inform the Government of the Republic of Croatia at least once a month about the application of the Decree, and individual reports will be adduced. The pursuing agents are bound to inform the Government of the Republic of Croatia via Ministry of Justice and Administration immediately about the irregularities perceived in implementing the Decree and about authority abuses, and to institute appropriate legal proceedings within its scope of competence.

6.   The Ministry of the Interior is bound, in compliance with law regulations, to undertake activities aimed at detection of perpetrators of criminal acts, and to institute appropriate legal proceedings before the competent prosecutor's offices. About pressures and illegal actions with regard to implementing its legal authorizations and especially about excluding perpetrators of criminal acts out of its control, the Ministry of the Interior is bound to inform immediately the pursuing bodies and the Government of the Republic of Croatia.

7.   Violations of citizen rights and liberties are to be solved primarily through judicial institutions. The Ministry of Justice and Administration will, in the framework of its regular authorizations, examine more intensively the well-foundedness of complaints concerning the operation of courts, to take steps for proper and timely execution of court jobs in compliance with the law and other regulations, and to monitor and analyze

functioning of courts, performance of judges; it will report the Government of the Republic of Croatia on all these findings every three months.

8. The Ministry of Justice and Administration will provide within its powers:
a) continuous operation of all judicial bodies of the Republic of Croatia on the whole territory of the Republic, with a special stress on the work of judicial bodies on the crisis-affected areas, applying also the institute of work mobilization for carriers of judicial functions;
b) correct application of decrees on functioning of the penal system of the Republic of Croatia in the conditions of the state of war or of the imminent danger for independence and integrity of the Republic of Croatia, and, when necessary, it will organize meetings and consultations, and render assistance to carriers of judicial functions in implementation of the said decrees.

9. The Ministry of Justice and Administration is bound to inform the Government of the Republic of Croatia immediately of every violation of the independence of the court authority, pressures exerted on carriers of judicial functions, and similar irregularities.

10. The Ministry of Defense will pass regulations in order to ensure the necessary discipline in Croatian army units, which will restrict strictly any movement outside barracks of soldiers who are not on battlefields. The Ministry of Defense will ensure, on local levels, compliance with the decisions of civil authorities and will forbid any interference of members of the armed formations of the Croatian Army in the wor k of civil bodies of authority.

11. All ministries are bound to reconsider the currently valid statutory orders with full force of the law, which the Government of the Republic of Croatia, on the basis of the proposals from some ministries, was proposing to the President of the Republic of Croatia, to analyze the experience in theirimplementation, and, depending on the results of the analysis, propose alterations and complements to, or withdrawal of, certain decrees or statutory orders.

On the basis of the adopted evaluations, judgements and conclusions, the Government of the Republic of Croatia obliges municipal and other executive bodies of authority in the Republic of Croatia to ensure, within their scope of competence, the implementation of these conclusions."

13. The Government of the Republic of Croatia has responded promptly also in connection with other crimes:
- murder of the members of the European Mission when their helicopter was shot down and attempt of murder of the members of the Mission who were in another helicopter which was attacked too;
- siege and destroying of Vukovar, Dubrovnik, Slunj, Kijevo, Voćin, Ćelije, and other Croatian towns and settlements, where the aim was to physically liquidate the local population;
- kidnapping of civilians (taken as hostages) to be used for exchange (Croatian side, in compliance with norms of the international law does not capture civilians):
- forcing soldiers of Croatian and Hungarian nationalities to participate in attacks on Croatian and Hungarian villages;

- holding in detention soldiers by the so-called JNA, who happened to be serving the Army at the time when the war broke out;
- expelling and forced moving away of Croatian population from Vojvodina, etc.

II.

The Government of the Republic of Croatia has considered with special care and in more detail the individual instances of violation of the laws of war and abuses of human liberties and rights stated in the letter of the US Helsinki Watch Committee dated February 13, 1992. The Government deeply appreciates the ideals that this Committee is striving at and the endeavour to protect human rights anywhere in the world, and it shares with the Committee these ideals and endeavour.

The Government of the Republic of Croatia wants to inform the public and the organization "Helsinki Watch" about the measures it has taken and it is taking to provide prerequisites to prevent instances of violations of human rights and to provide conditions for attaining durable peace on the territory of the Republic of Croatia and about measures taken in order to detect the perpetrators of the crimes.

When the new institutions of the democratic political system and institutions of the constitutional state were established, it was necessary to change lawful instruments and to ensure its implementation in new and complex political circumstances. The process of organizing the democratic state has been immensely made difficult by the aggression on the Republic of Croatia.

Instead of operations within its normal and usual scope of work, the police, as the only armed force, had to take the first burden in the defense of the state. Besides, the police itself, as the most delicate institution of the new democratic state, has to go through a process of personnel restructuring, so that it could get rid of the remnants of the former rgime and its political criteria.

In the Republic of Croatia has been developed a normative framework for functioning of the juridical system and of institutions of democratic political authority including the functioning in emergency circumstances. According to the Law on Defense, ("Narodne novine" /Official Gazette of the Republic of Croatia/, 53A/91 and 73/91), all the members of armed forces, where also special formations and reserve police corps of the Republic of Croatia are included, are obliged to observe the rules of the international law of war in the humane treatment of the enemy wounded and captured, the rules on protection of the population and other rules of this law in compliance with the Constitution of the Republic of Croatia, with laws and with the accepted liabilities based on the international law.

The President of the Republic has issued a Decree on Treatment of Persons Captured in War Conflicts, in which, in connection with the armed conflicts in the Republic of Croatia, the regulations of the Geneva Convention on treatment of the prisoners of war of August 24, 1949 are applied. The Ministry of Defense as well as some other services have issued quite a number of individual enactments that regulate the rules of procedure for members of the armed forces.

The President of the Republic has, on the proposal of the Government of the Republic of Croatia and which was subsequently corroborated by the Parliament, issued a Decree on Information Activities during Wartime with the aim to ensure a flow of information in the interest of the defense of the Republic of Croatia. The Decree was issued in the situation when the total telecommunication, television and radio broadcasting systems were destroyed by the aggressor according to a systematic plan, and the state television was reduced to only one program. The Ministry of Information intervened in accordance with the Decree only in one instance, when the data transmitted had a character of the military secret information, and it did not influence the freedom of information dissemination and press in other situations mentioned in the Helsinki Watch letter.

Please note that there is no one single country involved in war operations where there is no control over announcement of strategically important data.

The President of the Republic has on the proposal of the Government of the Republic of Croatia and which was subsequently corroborated by the Parliament, issued statutory orders with full force of the law whose aim is to ensure efficient operation of the state administration bodies and especially the judiciary and police.

Restrictiveness of the said regulations is commensurate to the conditions which prevailed in the Republic of Croatia till the discontinuation of hostilities by the end of 1991. The said regulations do not restrict human rights and liberties as anticipated by international treaties and conventions as well as by the Constitution, Constitutional Law on Human Rights and Liberties and on Rights of Ethnic and National Communities or Minorities and by other regulations of the Republic of Croatia. It has been found out in practical life that these regulations are applied very seldom, so that the Government has requested the competent ministries to examine the possibility of their repealing.

A system of military police, military investigation bodies and military judiciary has been organized in the Republic of Croatia. In all individual cases of violation of internationally accepted rules of law of the war and of other abuses and restrictions of human rights amd liberties, police or legal authorities have started procedures for establishing the acts and their committers. The data on individual cases mentioned in the Helsinki Watch letter are presented in the Annex.

The fact that the war aimed at conquering Croatian territories has been carried on exclusively on the territory of the Republic of Croatia is the reason for serious difficulties that the authority of the Republic of Croatia is confronted with. The incredible brutality of the conqueror, in the shape that has not been recorded in the recent war history of the world, and which is motivated with the physical liquidation of Croats as the people and of their cultural heritage on the areas which are desired to be annexed to Serbia, as well as a great military power of the enemy in comparison to incomparably poorer armed forces of the Republic of Croatia have unfortunately led to some serious instances of human rights abuses on the Croatian side, too. The Croatian Government shares the concern of Helsinki Watch with regard to human rights abuses that have taken place, and it uses all prerogatives of the executive power in order to ensure that these cases do not recur and the culprits be punished as they deserve.

126

The greatest number of cases mentioned in the Helsinki Watch letter refers to the regions which are neither beyond control of the Croatian authorities or are in zones of war conflicts. Since the majority of the offenses and crimes have been committed in the areas that were occupied or have been occupied still today, the majority of perpetrators are out of reach for the pursuing and judiciary bodies of the Republic of Croatia. It is impossible to carry out an investigation on the spot in the areas beyond control of the Croatian authorities, while in a zone involved in a conflict the investigations on the spot are carried out under very troublesome conditions and with exposure to great dangers, which must be taken into account when evaluating the efficiency of the work of investigating and court bodies, because they are simply not capable to act efficiently everywhere. Even in the cases when the facts or perpetrators of the crimes were available to pursuing bodies of the Republic of Croatia, the crime-detecting processing or investigation activities were performed in wartime circumstances, which often resulted in the impossibility of making the investigation on the spot, in the unavailability of the witness or in the impossibility to perform professional expertises. In this sense an indicative figure shows that the number of the detected perpetrators of criminal offenses on the territory under control of Croatian authorities is by 7 % higher in 1991 than in 1990.

As it was already pointed out before, the Government of the Republic of Croatia is aware of the fact that there are cases where internationally accepted rules of the law of war have been infringed and where human rights and liberties have been violated and abused, and, accordingly, corresponding legal proceedings have been initiated.

Some of the statements in the letter are, however, not well-founded on the verified data, which is substantiated in more detail in the Annex. For example, this refers to the case of Široka Kula, where is the identity of victims extremely doubtful or to the statement that 50 % of Serbs moved away from Zagreb, which is quite certainly not true.

We share the concern of Helsinki Watch Committee for the great number of the killed and wounded journalists. The data available to the Ministry of Interior show that Croatian forces are not responsible for the murder of any one journalist, which is also understandable because journalists, as the most important witnesses of war crimes in Croatia, have always had free access on the whole area under control of the Croatian authorities, while the access permitted by military Serbian authorities was often reserved only for Serbian journalists.

The statements referring to discrimination on ethnic basis in police forces are not comapatible with reality: nobody has been fired only because he is a Serb or a member of any other minority, and a number of Serbs employed with the police forces is even today still far above the percentage with which Serbs participate in the ethnic structure of the population in Croatia. It is also not true that people are dismissed from work because they are Serbs; the truth is, however, that part of the Serbs left their jobs of their own free will and included themselves in terrorist activities.

Harassments of citizens of Serbian nationality who are not included in terrorist actions nor have any connection with them are quite numerous, and the Ministry of the Interior has intervened in a series of cases. The implications of Helsinki Watch that indivudual citizens have been exposed to a lot of trouble because they criticized the Government are not well-founded, which can be seen best from the Croatian press, where there have been pieces of very severe criticism addressed to the Government or to individual officials but without any consequences for the authors of the texts. Some arbitrary actions by some individuals from the lower structure levels of authority are, however, not to exclude, but the Government can react only if it gets direct information from the affected persons. As for the doubts that the Croatian Government interferes in the activities of the judiciary and the doubts about political motives in Administration of Justice, they are not well-founded. The Croatian Government is a multi-party one (it is composed of HDZ /Croatian Democratic Union/, HKDS /Croatian Christian-Democratic Party/, HNS /Croatian People's Party/, SDP /Social Democratic Party/, SDSH /Croatian Social Democratic Party/, SSH /Croatian Socialist Party/ and until recently also HDS /Croatian Democratic Party/ and HSLS /Croatian Social Liberal Party/), and political orientations of its members are different. For instance, the Minister of Justice and Administration is a member of an oppositional party (HNS).

The Croatia Government is deeply concerned by the cases of missing persons in areas of war conflicts; the number of the reported missing Serbs in Gospi is much larger than the one mentioned by Helsinki Watch, i.e. 65, and, additionally, 39 missing Croats have also been reported. There have also been instances of robbery and of setting fire to houses of the Serbs who went over to the enemy side; these cases are being examined by the investigation bodies.

It is unacceptable that the methods used by the aggressor in his conquering acts of savagery are imitated on the Croatian side, regardless of how justified the fury against murderers and plunderers may be. We also fully agree with the statements of Helsinki Watch that the war that is carrying on in Croatia does not give any right to local authorities not to obey law regulations.

From the methodological point of view some objections can be made to the approach of Helsinki Watch. If it wants to deal with the history of the development of the conflict, then it is necessary to mention that the beginning of the conflict cannot be linked with the election campaign in Croatia. The causes are more profound, and their demonstration was recorded back in 1989, when in Knin, during the celebration of Kosovo battle, banners were displayed with the slogan "This is Serbia". The Government of the Republic of Croatia has been always ready for a dialogue and for negotiations for a peaceful coexistence. The response to the offer made to the leader of the Serbian Democratic Party (SDP), Jovan Rašković, to be Vice President of the Croatian Parliament were killings of the Croatian policemen and civilians, expelling of citizens of non-Serbian nationality but also of those Serbs who tried to protect their neighbours Croats, Hungarians, Czecks, Slovaks and others. In the formations of the Croatian army there are many citizens of Serbian nationality who fight, and often they even take very responsible positions.

Further, out of sight vanishes the fact, that an incredibly dirty war with a view to conquer territories has been unfortunately carried on on the ground of Croatia. The Government of the Republic of Croatian has been directing attention of the international public to this fact for a long time. In such a war to defend the country that the state of Croatia has been confronted with, often without possibilities to protect the civilian population from annihilation, it is not easy to preserve standards of ethical behaviour, morality and the level of freedom for an individual, which are only natural for a country living in peace. In Croatia the war is still going on, and the long-expected arrival of the United Nations peace-keeping troops should render possible that the war comes to the end.

The return of the displaced persons (expellees and refugees) which is rightly required by Helsinki Watch too, represents a vital interest of the Republic of Croatia and the most difficult task the Croatian authority has been facing. The aggression of Serbian forces has expelled about 15 % of the Croatian population from their homes, which makes a social control remarkably difficult and creates an unnatural social atmosphere which results in an increasing scope of criminal acts. An additional problem lies in the fact that on the occupied areas in the Republic of Croatia the inhabitants of the Croatian villages are still expelled every day and after that their villages are burned down, destroyed and even ploughed over by bulldozers.

The Croatian Government demands from the UN peace-keeping forces to render possible the return of all the refugees and expellees irrespective of their nationalities. Without the come back of the displaced persons to the places where they fled away or were expelled from, the UN mission would not execute its task, for which it has been set in motion.

In order to materialize the return of the expelled and refuged autochthonous population, it will be necessary to return new settlers who were settled from Serbia and other parts of Croatia by the authority of Serbia onto these areas in the course of the last year and this year.

The Government of the Republic of Croatia has started a procedure to review the status of the expellees and refugees and the program of returning for all the displaced persons, the process of reviewing and abolishing all restrictive statutory regulations with the force of the law passed in the course of the duration of the aggression, as well as the process of demobilization of reserve formations of the Croatian Army.

With implementation of the peace-keeping operations of the United Nations and establishment of peace on the integral territory of the sovereign state of Croatia, the Government of the Republic of Croatia will have completed the procedure of establishing facts, of pursuing and punishing of perpetrators of crimes aimed at violation of human rights and of other kinds of discrimination.

III.

The Government of the Republic of Croatia having deliberated upon the letter of Helsinki Watch dated February 13, 1992, and the reports received from the Ministry of Justice and Administration, Public Prosecutor's Office, Ministry of Defense, Ministry of the Interior and Ministry of Information with regard to this letter, and whereas

taking a firm position, that protection of the basic rights of man and citizen is one of the fundamental principles of the constitutional state and of the constitutional system of the Republic of Croatia,

129

referring to its continuous commitment to a peaceful solution of all issues, especially in its addresses to the Government of the Republic of Serbia,

stressing permanent attention with which it monitors observance of the law of war and of valid international conventions,

pointing to the considerably aggravated conditions for functioning of all government bodies, which are caused by the fact that the war has been carried on the ground of the Republic of Croatia only,

emphasizing its care for protection of people and property involved in war atrocities,

reminding of its statement of February 4, 1992,

appreciating any benevolent pointing to difficulties in development and functioning of democratic political institutions, in the light of experience and standards of the developed civil democracies,

passes the following

STATEMENT

1.   The Government of the Republic of Croatia, from the very beginning, condemned most severely any threatening of democratic political institutions and any violation of principles of the constitutional state, and especially violation of basic rights and liberties of man and citizen, irrespective of his national, religious or any other affiliation, and it demands from the competent bodies that perpetrators be ascertained and found.

2.   All the efforts taken by the United Nations, European Community, Conference on Security and Cooperation in Europe and other international organizations and institutions, aimed at consistent observance of rights of man and citizen, and at providing conditions for achieving lasting peace on the entire territory of the Republic of Croatia, are highly appreciated.

3.   The Government of the Republic of Croatia is addressing again to the international public with an invitation to all international non-governemtal and humanitarian organizations and institutions that deal with protection of human rights, and to legal experts, victimologists and scientists to send their observers or come themselves on the entire territory of the Republic of Croatia in order to obtain a direct insight into the state of conditions and observance of human rights.

4.   The United Nations, European Community and Conference on Security and Cooperation in Europe, as well as other international organizations and institutions are requested to support the demand of the Republic of Croatia for establishment of an

international court of law for war crimes committed on the territory of the Republic of Croatia.

5.   The United Nations, European Community and Conference on European Security and Cooperation, as well as the governments of these organizations are requested to found a commission that would be sent here along with the UN peace-keeping forces, which would objectively and impartially ascertain facts and pieces of evidence regarding war crimes on the territory of the Republic of Croatia.

6.   The Government of the Republic of Croatia holds the silence of the international public and international organizations in charge of protection of human rights unacceptable with regard to all the more mass occurrences of forced evacuation and expelling of the Croatian population from the occupied regions of the Republic of Croatia, in the Republic of Serbia and Republic of Bosnia and Herzegovina.

7.   The Government of the Republic of Croatia points particularly to the existence of concentration camps on the territory of the Republic of Serbia and on the temporarily occupied areas of the Republic of Croatia, where captured civilians have been detained and tortured (the most ill-famed concentration camp is located in the coal mines of Aleksinac).

8.   The Government of the Republic of Croatia wants also to draw attention to demolishing of non-Serbian settlements on the temporarily occupied areas of the Republic of Croatia and to wrecking of original registry documentation for the purpose of altering the demographic picture of the population.

9.   The Government of the Republic of Croatia is sending an appeal to international organizations to stop and prevent a further genocide over the Croatian population.

10.   The Government of the Republic of Croatia is addressing the international public and requesting representatives of all international governmental and non-governmental organizations and institutions that deal with the protection of the environment to send their observers or to come personally onto the integral territory of the Republic of Croatia in order to obtain a direct insight into serious disruptions of environmental values and the extent of the ecological damages incurred.

11.   In accordance with its democratic approach, the Government of the Republic of Croatia has been directing consistently and persistently attention to the problems in functioning of the constitutional state. The Government of the Republic of Croatia states that a series of measures has successfully been implemented in this sense:

- reinstatement of forces assigned for interior affairs (police) from defensive tasks back to their original regular duties has already led to an increasing efficiency in protection of citizens from all kinds of mistreatment on the areas under the control of the Croatian authorities;

- forming of military police formations, which ensures control of movement of armed persons and makes actions of paramilitary organizations fully impossible;

- with intensified efforts of the investigation and court bodies, all cases where there is a well-founded suspicion of a criminal act having been committed have been prosecuted.

12.   For the purpose of providing conditions for further democratization of the society, all ministries are obliged to reconsider the valid statutory orders with full force of the law that the Government of the Republic of Croatia, on the proposal of the ministries, submitted to the President of the Republic of Croatia for adopting. After they have analyzed anew the reasons for passing this orders and their efficiency in implementation, the ministries will suggest that these orders be retained in force, alternated or supplemented, or that they be called off, till March 7,1992 at the latest.

13.   The Ministry of Defense and the Ministry of the Interior are bound to act in a preventive manner and to examine the compliance of activities of the members of its bodies with legal deeds of the Republic of Croatia and with the norms of the law of war.

14.   The Ministry of Justice and Administration is, within the scope of its regular authorizations, bound to accelerate the solving of cases of human rights abuses, to examine more intensively well-foundedness of complaints regarding the work of courts of law, to take measures for proper and timely carrying out of court jobs in compliance with the law and other regulations, and in this sense to monitor and analyze the functioning of the courts and work of the judges.

15.   The Ministry of Justice and Administration will prepare, until the next session of the Government, its proposal for the foundation of a Commission for Gathering Data Referring to War Crimes Committed in the Republic of Croatia.

President of the Government of the Republic of Croatia

Dr. Franjo Gregurić

132

TO THE STANDPOINTS OF THE GOVERNMENT OF THE REPUBLIC OF CROATIA ON OBSERVATION OF HUMAN RIGHTS AS THE RESPONSE TO THE LETTER OF THE U.S. HELSINKI WATCH COMMITTEE DATED FEBRUARY 13, 1992

The cases considered by Helsinki Watch are categorized in five sections in this Supplement:

I.   Rules of War Violations
II. Discrimination on National and Political Basis
III. Restrictions on the Freedom of the Press and Expression
IV. Interference with the Independence of the Judiciary

I. RULES OF WAR VIOLATIONS

1. A SURVEY OF CRIME STATISTICS IN THE REPUBLIC OF CROATIA

Intentional destruction of civilian property by bombs or other explosive devices, apart from combat activities, has been constantly increasing and is a subject of police investigation. During the period between August 18 (the date when the armed rebellion started) and December 31, 1990, records indicate that 72 explosive devices were deliberate planted, and there was one case of arson. In 1991, these figures climbed to 1,871 explosions and 258 cases of arson. In the single month of January, 1992, as many as 243 explosions and 50 cases of arson were reported. In 1991, 1,557 criminal charges for such acts of terrorism were filed with law enforcement authorities, while penal proceedings were instituted against 1,402 suspects for terrorism and other grave criminal acts.

These figures primarily cover the area under the control of the Croatian authorities. In the data we have, cases of destruction of property number 1,500 for Serbian property, over 400 for Croatian property, and 50 for property of other ethnic groups. Due to the war circumstances, most offenders of these crimes have not yet been tracked down. According to police data concerning 100 criminals who have been identified, 84 are ethnic Croats, 13 Serbs, and 6 belong to other ethnic groups.

The number of cases of destruction of property belonging to the citizens of Croatian nationality in the temporarily occupied areas is several times greater, but there are no final data available, since the Croatian authorities do not have access to these areas.

The number of murders is increasing. During 1991, 437 murder cases were reported, which more than tripled the number from 1990 (137). The increase is mostly due to war crimes, although "classical" motives, such as marital and property disputes, alcoholism, and mental derangement are also present. Most victims are Croats. Final figures are expected to be much higher, but they will be known when normal conditions for police investigation will be met.

2. SUMMARY EXECUTIONS OF CIVILIANS AND PERSONS HORS DE COMBAT

The Helsinki Watch letter cites three major incidents of this type: in Karlovac, Gospić, and Marino Selo (in the Pakrac district).

2.1. Karlovac, September 21

13 prisoners of war were killed and 2 more fired upon, (one of whom was injured), on September 21, in connection with combat activities in the area and the capture of prisoners near Karlovac, at the bridge over the Korana river. After an investigation conducted by the Croatian police, a warrant (no. 321/91) has been put out for the arrest of the crime's leading suspect, policeman Mihajlo Hrastov, who is on the run[1]. An official police report on this case was sent to the Amnesty International Office in London in the second half of November.

2.2 Gospić, probably Mid-October

The Helsinki Watch letter reports disappearances of a number of Serbs from Gospić, and connects this with 24 burned bodies found near the villages of ŠirokaKula and Perušić, in the Lika region, and five more bodies discovered nearby.

In order to understand the problems of the police investigation in Gospić and the seriousness with which it is being conducted, it should be mentioned that the number of citizens reported missing of Serbian nationality is far greater than the number mentioned by the Helsinki Watch report, namely, 65. In addition to this, 39 citizens of Croatian nationality have also disappeared, 9 of whom are suspected to be held in prison by Serbian irregulars in Lički Novi Osik.

Gospić suffered fierce attacks, and at one point even half of the town was occupied. A certain number of Serbian citizens of Gospić left the town just before the unexpected all-out attack on Gospić, which made it more difficult to find out whether all disappeared persons were the victims of violence or whether they voluntarily left the town to the area temporarily occupied by the irregular Serbian authorities. For example, one of the missing persons, Djuro Pavlica, is reported to have been seen in the Knin prison.

The Croatian police expressed doubts concerning the connection between the discovered bodies and the Gospić disappearances reported by Helsinki Watch, as well as suspicions about the pathologist's reports. The Croatian police had no access to the site where the bodies were found, the bodies themselves, nor the pathologist's reports.

In the Široka Kula area, a village in the Lika region, whole families of Croatian nationality, who did not manage to take refuge from the area, were massacred during September. 13 Croats were killed, their bodies burned, and 5 more were injured on one day, September 25. The fate of 18 other Croats (men and women) from this village has not been cleared, although they may be in the prison of Lički Osik.

---

[1]Latest information (11.03.1992.) from the Minstry of the Interior is that Mihajlo Hrastov has two days ago been arrested.

The identification of the massacred bodies from ŠirokaKula requires special skill in pathological expertise, because two months have passed since the massacre occured and the bodies were burned. Croatian Police experts hold the report made by the Belgrade pathologist, Dr Stamenković, unacceptable according to professional police criminology standards, because the autopsy was not conducted under the surveillance of neutral pathologists, while the details of the investigation, of the autopsy, and of the procedures used to identify the bodies were not submitted to the Croatian police. The pathologist's report on one hand mentions specific methods of brutal execution, such as knife stabbing, bayonette or axe wounds inflicted to the forehead, and shots at close range and on the other it states that the bodies were discovered approximately two months after being soaked with gasoline and burned. Since in this area Croats have been killed since late August, when the territory was occupied by the Serbian troops, there is a possibility that the found bodies were the bodies of the Croats reported missing.

The Croatian police informed the Government that after a long and extensive investigation, they have enough material to successfully conclude the investigation in the near future.

2.3 Marino Selo (Pakrac), November 15-25

According to the Helsinki Watch letter, the Croatian Army soldiers captured 15 Serbs from the village of Kip, 6 from the village of Klisa, and 1 from the village of Batinjani, on November 15. These 22 persons were imprisoned in a hotel in Marino Selo and were exposed to severe physical maltreatment. 14 of them were eventually killed, and 3 persons were reported released in an exchange of prisoners on December 12, after their incarceration in several different prisons. Helsinki Watch does not report what happened to the remaining five.

During this time, combat activity was going on in the districts of Pakrac and Daruvar, and the Croatian police had neither control nor jurisdiction over this territory. The Croatian police had no previous information on this case. The Croatian police considers the Helsinki Watch statement to be an official initiative for implementation of criminal proceedings, and the Ministry of the Interior has taken the necessary legal measures. Helsinki Watch will be notified on the established facts.

2.4 (Un)explained Deaths of Serbs

As it was noticed by Helsinki Watch, it seems that the police investigation of the murder of Srbislav Petrov from Umag, on September 5, 1991, was successfully concluded. Charges were brought against seven suspects, a warrant was issued for the arrest of an eighth.

Five persons are charged with the murder of Mihajlo, Marija, and Aleksandra Zec in Zagreb.

Helsinki Watch called upon the Croatian government to conduct a thorough investigation and to prosecute any found guilty, for what they call *unexplained deaths* of a number of Sisak citizens of Serbian nationality.

135

The Croatian police is investigating all the cases that were reported to the police headquarters in Sisak, and which Helsinki Watch mentioned in their letter. Some of these cases have been successfully concluded, while in others the offenders have not yet been identified.

A member of the Sisak police reserve forces was arrested, on suspicion of having committed the murder of Ilija Martić, which occurred on August 26, 1991, in the local pub "Viktorija."

Criminal procedures against unknown persons are underway concerning the cases of the Vila family, Vlado Bošić, Milenko Djapo, Zoran Vranešević, Miloš Čalić, and Jovo Crnobrnja.

Four Croatian soldiers were arrested, suspected of the murder of Damjan Zilić, and await trial at the military court in Zagreb.

The Helsinki Watch letter places the case of Branko Oljača among the unexplained. However, he has not appeared at his job at the Police Headquarters in Sisak since August 23, 1991. Since he did not return his weapons and gear, and nobody reported him missing, it is believed that he joined the Serbian irregular units in the Glina district.

A police investigations are being conducted for other cases mentioned in the Helsinki Watch letter.

In addition to the Sisak crimes cited by Helsinki Watch, in the Novska district a police investigation is drawing to a close on three murder cases, involving 11 victims. 8 Croatian soldiers held suspect have been arrested.

A request for investigation has been raised with the Osijek District Attorney concerning three crimes. 2 Croatian soldiers and one unidentified person are held suspect for the murders of 5 persons.

3. FAILURE TO PROSECUTE A KILLING

Helsinki Watch called upon the Croatian authorities *to investigate, arrest and charge those responsible* for the murder of Josip Reichl Kir on July 1, 1991, in Tenja.

The Croatian police considers that Ante Gudelj fired upon Josip Reichl Kir's car, and after killing Kir and two other passengers, escaped from the site of crime. An international warrant for his arrest was also issued by Osijek authorities, since he is suspected to have been abroad for some time. Upon capture, the Croatian government intends to pursue his extradition to Croatia, where he will brought to court and face trial for the murder of Kir and the two other persons.

4. TORTURE AND MISTREATMENT IN DETENTION

The Croatian authorities are deeply concerned about the descriptions of individual

136

plights of people who claim to have been mistreated and even tortured in jail. With regard to the circumstances in which the documentation has been collected, while the descriptions may be accurate, it is doubtful that these testimonies are typical. The Croatian Ministry of the Interior does not have detention centers or camps for internees. There are prisons (which all humanitarian, and all other international organizations can visit whenever they decide to; and some of the organizations actually visited them), as well as holding facilities on police headquarters premises. We take pride in our efforts to create humane living conditions in our prisons. We must point out that when we exchange prisoners, the physical condition of those we give away is usually much better than that of the prisoners we get.

It is important that respect for the law and humane norms of behavior be implemented throughout our law enforcement system.

The military and police authorities have been ordered to investigate the cases of mistreatment in jails considered by Helsinki Watch. In the case of maltreatment in the Sisak Police Headquarters (Josip K. and his brother) the Ministry of the Interior considers the Helsinki Watch statement to be a criminal charge. We appeal to Helsinki Watch to provide us with the names of persons who were maltreated in order to facilitate the investigations and thus solve this problem where the mistreatment has taken place.

In the case of the alleged mistreatment of Djordje Rkman, he did not report that he had been maltreated by the police. According to the witness, Mijo Lončarević from Kovrivna, who recently managed to escape from this predominantly Serb village, Rkman, after he had been released in an exchange of prisoners, became the head of the so-called "territorial police" (in the communist regime Rkman was one of the leading police officers), and he was especially active in war crimes and looting.

5. ARBITRARY ARRESTS AND DISAPPEARANCES

In the case of Dragan Rajšić, Sisak, there are contradictory data on the manner and time of disappearance. Further inquiries are underway, although the data on the suspects are lacking.

According to the report of the Military Police, Col. Vasilije Kovač, arrested at Široka Kula, was held in the Kerestinec prison. After being questioned about his connections with Serbian irregulars in territories which are not under the control of Croatian authorities, Kovač was released.

6. TAKING CIVILIAN PRISONERS

We appreciate Helsinki Watch for drawing attention to the international conventions forbidding the use of civilians/hostages for prisoner exchanges with the enemy, who does not respect these norms. Croatia does not use civilians/hostages for prisoner exchanges, which is also indicated by the fact that Croatian side presently holds only about 200 prisoners, while the Serbian side holds over 8,500 prisoners. It is estimated that 72% are civilians who are confined in some 40 prisons and camps, some of which are real concentration camps.

Croatian authorities have sent numerous appeals to the Yugoslav Army, to show humanity and to respect of the international conventions, but without success. Especially cruel was the abduction of the wounded from the Vukovar hospital, and concealing them before the International Red Cross.

7. DESTRUCTION OF CIVILIAN PROPERTY AND ROBBERY

Helsinki Watch claimed that *Serbian property has intentionally been destroyed by individual Croats or members of the Croatian police or army.* It is already widely known that, throughout Croatia, civilian propery suffered extensive damage during the war. Apart from damage caused in combat, there was a large number of incidents in which civilian property was intentionally damaged or destroyed. Although the overwhelming majority of cases involved Croatian property, cases of looting and damage of Serbian property, were also registered. In the territory controlled by the Croatian authorities, about 30% of the damaged property is owned by Croats, about 60% by Serbs, and about 10% by members of other ethnic groups. The Croatian police is investigating each reported case, regardless of the nationality of the injured party.

The Croatian police has also taken extensive precautionary measures to prevent vandalism and looting. As a result of the completed investigations, as of January 29, 1992 Croatian police suspects 103 identified persons to be responsible for these criminal acts. Further action and proper trials are expected to follow in the aforementioned cases. In many cases, the criminal proceedings are already underway.

We consider the claims that Croatian authorities are not active enough in the prevention of the destruction of civilian property unfair. It is necessary to point out that in Croatia the war is going on, and that, under such circumstances, one cannot expect that the effectiveness concerning penal proceedings, tracing down suspects, and prevention of criminal activities, can match the usual standards at times of peace.

It should be noticed, that discipline of the Croatian soldiers has been significantly improved since the Military police was organized within the Croatian Army.

8. ARBITRARY SEARCHES AND SEIZURES

According to the Croatian legal acts in vigour, searches without warrant are illegal. Accordingly, if searches without warrant were conducted, such acts are illegal, and the offenders must be made responsible for breaking the law. The Government has warned the ministries concerned, about the possibility of such illegal acts and required that the law be strictly respected.

The Croatian government cannot discuss the issue of justifiability of searches of entire villages. It is well known that the Yugoslav Army and the Republic of Serbia had been systematically arming the citizens of Serbian nationality on the territory of the Republic of Croatia, long before the war broke out. The fact that entire villages were armed in this way, even with heavy weapons, is also known to Helsinki Watch. Thus it is not surprising that police, after so many murder cases have been committed, is strictly controlling the possession of weapons.

138

9. KILLINGS, ASSAULT AND HARASSMENT OF JOURNALISTS

We share Helsinki Watch's concern about the large number of journalists who have been killed, wounded, and physically or otherwise attacked while reporting on the war in Croatia. Unfortunately, as of February 22, 1992, the death toll is even higher then the one mentioned in the Helsinki Watch report. According to the most recent data of the Ministry of Information, 22 journalists have been killed[2] while covering the war in Croatia.[3] Although protected by the Geneva Conventions, and clearly identified by their "Press" signs, journalists reporting from the Croatian side of the front line have often been deliberately targeted.[4]

The Helsinki Watch report mentions specifically the case of Zoran Midžić, Bora Petrović, Dejan Miličević and Sreten Ilić who were killed *under circumstances in which Croatian forces may have been responsible.* The incident, however, took place on the territory which was not under the control of the Croatian Army, and several Croatian Army officials have reported that the Croatian forces were not involved in any combat activities in the area at the time of the incident.[5] The area is still out of the control of Croatian forces, and therefore no evidence which could specify the cause of death of the journalists is accessible

---

[2]This number includes two Russian journalists, Viktor Nogin and Genadij Kurinoj, who are still missing, but believed dead, see below.

[3] Cf "Journalist' Death Toll High in Yugoslavia", **New York Times**, January 29,1992. "More journalists have died covering the first seven months of fighting in Yugoslavia than in an equal period in any war in recent memory... The death toll for journalists is high because, unlike the Persian Gulf war, for example, where reporters' movements were tightly restricted, the Yugoslav combat zones are readily accessible to the press." We must note that the liberty of movement in the combat areas is respected primarily on the Croatian side of the frontline. The other side, however, permits group visits under strict military control.

[4]"It's Open Season on Journalists", **Chicago Tribune**, January 9, 1992, by Storer H. Rowley. "Early on, journalists covering the Yugoslav conflict ended the usual practice of clearly marking their vehicles with "PRESS" or "TV" signs, because often this actually attracted fire."

[5] Cf. "They killed their journalists", **Jedinstvo** (Sisak), October 17, 1991. "The representative of the Croatian National Guard for Sisak and Banija denied any responsibility of the Croatian Army for the deaths of the Belgrade journalists, explaining that (according also to the Belgrade press) the death of the journalists occurred on the territory which is controlled jointly by the Yugoslav Army and Serbian terrorists. He stated that Croatian forces, in the area under their control, throughout Wednesday (October 9th) were not involved in any combat operations, nor did they fire upon anyone. On the territory controlled by the Croatian Defense there was no reported movement of journalists, so the HQ of Sisak and Banija have no information when and how the journalists were killed."
"The Banija frontline kills journalists", **Novice**, October 11,1991. The Slovenian paper states that "Belgrade accused "criminal Ustashe hands" for the deaths of the four journalists, though the journalists were on the territory controlled by the Yugoslav Army."

to the Croatian authorities. However, there are indications that their car hit a land mine. Croatian Ministry of the Interior excludes every possibility that journalists were killed by Croatian forces.

According to witnesses, Radio Vukovar journalists Siniša Glavašević and Branimir Polovina were taken to an unknown destination by the Yugoslav Army soldiers after the fall of Vukovar on November 19, 1991. Siniša Glavašević, who was wounded in the beginning of November, was removed with 250 other injured persons from the Vukovar hospital by YA soldiers before The Red Cross was allowed to enter the hospital.[6]

Neither his nor Polovina's name has appeared on any exchange list offered by the Yugoslav Army, which refuses to give any information concerning their whereabouts or fates.

The evidence gathered by the Croatian Ministry of the Interior suggests that two other missing journalists, Viktor Nogin and Genadij Kurinoj, were killed near the village of Panjane on September 2, 1991 when their car was hit by a grenade fired from a shoulder-held grenade launcher in the vicinity of the Serbian irregulars' ambush. The village was not under the control of Croatian forces at the time of the incident. Photographs of the missing journalists were published several times in all Croatian newspapers, as part of the effort to gather as much evidence as possible about their disappearance[7]. Croatian police forces have been working in cooperation with investigators from Russia since the beginning of the inquiry.[8] In a meeting that is expected to take place in Pecs (Hungary), all parties involved (the Croatian Police, the Russian investigators and the YA) will present existing evidence in order to precisely establish what happened to the missing journalists.

II. DISCRIMINATION ON NATIONAL AND POLITICAL BASIS

The Croatian government shares Helsinki Watch's concern about full protection of the civil and human rights of individuals and groups without any kind of distinction, such as ethnic origin or political conviction. There have been some cases of individual incidents, threatening and harassment of the citizens of Serbian nationality in the non-occupied territory of Croatia with mixed ethnic structure.

---

[6] Cf "We are all Vukovar", **Večernji list** , November 26, 1991. "(Siniša Glavašević) was to be evacuated with the wounded... meanwhile the occupation soldiers entered Vukovar's hospital before the arrival of the ICRC. 250 wounded persons were taken in an unknown direction. Siniša was among them."

[7] Cf "Secret of the Blue Omega", **Večernji list** , February 1st, 1992. and "Where are the Russian journalists", **Dnevnik**, January 9, 1992.

[8] The Croatian Police recently received a letter of thanks from the Russian authorities for their   extensive assistance in the inquiry into the disappearance of the two Russian journalists.

The Croatian Government takes a clear stand on that matter and the Government cannot be made responsible for the criminal acts committed by individual citizens. However, in respect to the protection of citizens against such abuses, much can certainly be improved. The greatest hinderance to the establishment of the public order and peace is the continuing aggression which is been led against Croatia. Such incidents will decrease substantially upon the arrival of the United Nations peacekeeping troops and once the aggression is terminated.

1. HARASSMENT AND DISCRIMINATION OF CITIZENS

As an example of harassment, Helsinki Watch refers to informative conversations which police officers had with professor Svetozar Livada, and interprets them as an attempt of pressure on his political group - Serbian Democratic Forum. The Government cannot comment on single cases of police investigations with similar background. It should be noted - and indeed it is, by Helsinki Watch itself - that at times of war it is extremely difficult to discuss issues such as defense needs or the plausibility of every step taken by the bodies in authority in such situations.

It is necessary to mention that the President of the Serbian Democratic Forum took part in The Hague Conference as a representative in the Croatian delegation. His political group, in full freedom, engages both in Zagreb and throughout the country, in a significant amount of activity, often very critically colored towards the Croatian government. Therefore, it does not seem appropriate to impute to the Croatian authorities far-reaching hidden intentions on the basis of the example of professor Livada.

However, the proportions of the problem are considerably greater than what could be concluded from the Helsinki Watch letter. In a society, which inherited a milieu lacking certain social norms and responsibilities, violations of human integrity occur in a greater number and sometimes are more serious than those which attracted the attention of Helsinki Watch, which was observing the circumstances from a different angle and from a different cultural environment.

It must be pointed out that the statement that half of the Zagreb citizens of Serbian nationality fled in fear of harassment, or due to harassment, is fully untrue.

2. DISCRIMINATION IN THE WORKPLACE

The Croatian government, as Helsinki Watch correctly stated, promptly reacted to the signing of "loyalty oaths" of the citizens of Serbian nationality, and such cases have not been repeated afterwards. The Office for Relations Between Etnic Groups is carrying out an investigation of the individual cases, in which there is reason to believe that the injured party lost the job because of nationality. However, due to a heavy recession which has along with the war hit Croatia, it is difficult to confirm that someone lost the job because of national discrimination.

3. DISCRIMINATION IN THE POLICE FORCE

Helsinki Watch overlooked the fact that Croatia, after the free democratic elections of 1990, has come out of the communist regime. The main instrument of repression in the old system was the police force, whose members were persons absolutely loyal to the regime and its national composition included, as the Helsinki Watch letter cites, 75% of Serbs. Although the full legitimate right of the new authorities was to dismiss all those who were working for the police in the old regime, which was the practice in other ex-communist countries, this was not done. The police force was simply filled with new people.

According to the data of the Ministry of the Interior, from the democratic elections (middle 1990) to mid February 1992, as many as 6,873 employees of the Croatian Ministry of the Interior left their positions. 1,212 Serbs and 1,502 Croats left the police of their own accord. As many as 1,663 employees were dismissed, out of whom Serbs accounted for only 1.5%. Among those who were dismissed for insubordination, 556 were Croats and 853 Serbs. Among those who had to leave their position because of disciplinary violations, Serbs accounted for 45.5%. Among those who retired from active service, 750 were Serbs and 523 Croats. A total of 2,943 Serbs, 2,913 Croats, and 768 Yugoslavs were dismissed or left of their own accord. Nobody, however, was dismissed out of national discrimination. In addition to the statements in the Helsinki Watch letter base on the talks with Deputy Ministers of the Interior, herewith should be added false sick leaves, which some of the active members of the police force took, in order to join the ranks of Serbian irregulars. For instance, as many as 161 employees of the Sisak Police Headquarters joined the enemy ranks, whereas it is needless to mention the police forces in Knin and other districts, which are under control of the Yugoslav Army and Milan Martić, where all the policemen, voluntarily or forcefully, joined the enemy ranks.

III. RESTRICTIONS ON THE FREEDOM OF THE PRESS AND EXPRESSION

Helsinki Watch writes that *"the war has had a devastating effect on the freedom of the press"*. The Presidential decree "on war information", signed on October 30, 1991, is said to have introduced not only military censorship, but also (civilian) censorship panels at both the state and local level.

1. MILITARY CENSORSHIP

Helsinki Watch criticizes the Croatian government for having *"failed to prove that the press has in any way obstructed military operations or endangered national security"*. We share the view that military censorship is by no means a suitable step in developing a democracy, but we see it as an important tool for defending the one we have. Practically all countries in war find it necessary to censor military news.

The Croatian government has, however, chosen to almost completely dispense with censorship. Domestic and foreign correspondents have practically no other limitations in their work but the obligation to obtain, when they wish to visit the front line, a written permit from the regional defense command. Their access to the front line has, in essence, been unlimited[9]. There is a blatant difference between such a system and the "managed news"

---

[9] - Cf. Article by Michael Emery, Village Voice, January 23, 1992

concept used, for example, in the U.N. operation Desert Storm.

While we appreciate the motives of Helsinki Watch opposing in principle any military censorship, even in times of war, the Croatian Government does not find the position taken overly realistic.

Helsinki Watch is incorrect in surmising that our primary concern is to keep secret the number of casualties - quite on the contrary, the Croatian government regularly publishes a detailed and updated account of casualties (civilian/military, regions, age etc). Those who are not familiar with the procedure of how the casualties are defined, can easily be confused by the relatively low number of casualties (3,169). This number, namely, includes only those cases where all relevant data about the cause and circumstances of death are known, in accordance with the regulations of the World Medical Organization. In cases when the obligatory data cannot be established, the dead persons are considered missing (about 12,000), although for the majority of them, they are known to be dead.

Particularly in the initial stages of the aggression, the Croatian media did, unfortunately, provide many examples of how military secrets or sensitive defense information can inadvertently be passed to the enemy and cause substantial human and material loss.[10] Helsinki Watch representatives would have been informed about this had they contacted the Croatian Ministry of Information. Failure to do so deprived them of other relevant information as well.

2. "CIVILIAN CENSORSHIP"

In addition to the need of defending military secrets, the Government also faced the problem of counteracting the effects of psychological warfare in the media. It resisted, however, the temptation to introduce classical censorship to accomplish this task. In a series of interviews in the Croatian press, and in contacts with foreign diplomats at the time the decree was issued, the Information Minister made clear that the Government had no intention of using this form of censorship.[11]

---

[10] Cf. Ines Sabalić in **Nedjeljna Dalmacija**, November 14, 1991: "The need for military censorship exists: to publish in the newspapers that Tordinci is a reserve communication for Vukovar (and this happened a month and a half ago, while Tordinci was lost recently) was a crime out of negligence. The enemy staff read the story and overtook Tordinci, which greatly worsened the Vukovar situation. So, let us not publish from the field anything that damages the defense of Croatia. It should not be published that a village on the front line (as was the case) is defended by eight fighters when the enemy thought there were hundred times more".
Tihomir Dujmović (**Novi List**, December 7, 1991) arguing for the need of war censorship recalls, for example, a TV-program in which a reporter pointed out the most vulnerable part of a nuclear power plant..

[11] "Even if we wanted to introduce classical censorship, we would not be able to do it because we do not have people for it, and we do not have the organization. It would be the most single-minded bureaucracy which would lead us nowhere" (Branko Salaj interviewed by Ines SabaliÊ, Nedjeljna Dalmacija (Split), November 14, 1991). Similar statements by Mr. Salaj, for example, appeared in **Novi List** (Rijeka), December 7, 1991, and in the weekly

Instead, a new institution, the Information HQ of the Republic of Croatia, was formed to offer guidance and background information to the editors-in-chief of the major daily and weekly publications in the country. The government designated four ministers from different parties as IHQ members, who came from the Croatian Democratic Union, Croatian Democratic Party, Croatian Social Democratic Party and the Party of Democratic Change (reformed Communists). When the CDP-member resigned from the government (and the party), the Cabinet appointed, as a replacement, its Serbian member, who holds no party affiliations. The other three members were appointed by the Information Minister, chosen among journalists of high reputation who, by their inclinations, further diversified the field of political opinions.

The IHQ functions as an advisory body: it has no staff and its members meet on an *ad hoc*-basis. It has met several times with the editors-in-chief of the major news media. These meetings were, in fact, informal discussions on the problems of information activities encountered by the country and its media.

The Information Ministry has never used the powers imposed on them by the presidential decree, except in one instance when the circulation of the 94th issue of a sensationalist weekly, **Slobodni tjednik** was banned. This publication is singled out in the Helsinki Watch letter (p.15) as one of the main culprits in what is described as harassment by the media of members of the Serbian community in Croatia.

The banned issue of **ST** contained transcripts of telephone conversations between a commanding officer and the Head of the General Defense Staff, the Minister of Defense and the President of the Republic respectively. Official conversations of this nature are regarded as militarily secret, and their publication is prohibited.

The President of the Republic has proposed to the Government that he expects that the decree on "war information" be rescinded as soon as the U.N. peace-keeping force has been deployed.

The statement by Helsinki Watch that "*the Croatian government -both at the state and local levels - is trying to silence critical or independent publications through intimidation and economic pressure*" is one which bears little resemblance to reality.

The Croatian government, naturally, cannot exclude the possibility that certain individuals at different levels of the political establishment may have such ideas. The fact is, however, that practically all daily and weekly publications dating from the communist regime continue to be published. Newly begun periodicals are very few, those serious in their approach to politics even fewer. The party in power in Croatia, the Croatian Democratic Union (HDZ), publishes a weekly with very limited circulation. Apart from a few exceptions, most journalists continued writing for the same publications they did during the communist regime. Many exercise a critical approach toward each step taken by the new Government. There are also cases of intentional misinformation and conscious attempts to discredit the

---

Studio, at the end of November 1991. In an interview, made by Gojko Marinković in **Danas** (Zagreb), September 17, 1991, Minister Salaj affirmed there would not be any censorship unless Croatia was drawn into a total war: "Even then it seems to me that, if you look at the present world and its interrelated communications, censorship is a rather antiquated thing. Even (the United States of) America has problems with censorship."

Government.

Trying to support its unfounded statement that an official campaign had been undertaken against various publications in the news media, which constitutes "a serious detriment to the freedom of the press in Croatia", Helsinki Watch cites the case of **Slobodna Dalmacija**, a Split-based daily newspaper.

The Croatian government's attempt to prevent the privatization of **Slobodna Dalmacija** had economic, and not political motivation. That is to say, the process of privatization of **Slobodna Dalmacija** started before the appropriate legislation existed. Solvent firms tried to quickly sell their property, which usualy led to the private financial advantage of the managers. This issue was finally resolved in January 1992, when the court accepted an appeal by **Slobodna Dalmacija** and dismissed a previous decision by the Croatian Ministry of Justice to ban their privatization.

Helsinki Watch also misinterpreted the case of Mr Marko Bitanga, a local HDZ leader. Mr Bitanga competed for the position of director of **Slobodna Dalmacija** in August 1990, not in May 1991, as stated by Helsinki Watch. Therefore, it was nine months after his nomination that he strongly criticized the daily because it held President Tudjman responsible for calling citizens to demonstrate in front of the building of the Yugoslav Army Command in Split, while the president never called for such an action. A Yugoslav Army draftee was killed in this demonstration, which later resulted in very serious consequences. **Slobodna Dalmacija** has received a great deal of criticism since then, including some by a Croatian Parliament member, cited in the letter by Helsinki Watch. However, the Croatian government insists on full freedom of the press, knowing that market laws are the best indicators of objectiveness of the press, and believing that a newspaper continuously publishing false allegations cannot keep its readership.

As mentioned in the Helsinki Watch letter, the Croatian government has undertaken a number of steps to privatize former state enterprises, including the media. Helsinki Watch has shown concern that, as a part of this process, the Croatian Government is using economic means to close publications that are critical to the Government. Helsinki Watch mentions the weekly **Danas** as one targeted for closure because of its "independent and critical editorial policy". While recognizing that the journal had financial difficulties, Helsinki Watch mistakenly believes that it has been treated differently than other Vjesnik publications. The Government cannot be held responsible for the decision of the Vjesnik printing company to refuse further service to a publication which had extensive delays in payment and an extremely bleak market prospect, with sales reportedly plunging from more than 100,000 to only 24,000 copies within a year. The Croatian Government, in fact, tried to ensure a financial support to the weekly. On October 17, 1991, the Croatian Government gave the guarantees for a credit of 11,000,000 dinars (cca 275,000 DEM) to **Danas** with Zagrebačka banka (Zagreb Bank).[12]

Helsinki Watch claims that *the Croatian government has also taken steps to curb freedom of expression*, and bases its evidence on the case of Mirjana Jakelić, President of the Croatian chapter of the League of Communists - Movement for Yugoslavia (unregistered in Croatia). Charges against her were brought in the beginning of June 1991, at the District

---

[12] Cf "Who gets financed by the Croatian government", **Glasnik**, November 1, 1991.

Court in Zagreb.

Helsinki Watch states that Mirjana Jakelić was charged under Article 197(1) of the Croatian Criminal Code with "willfully spreading false rumors". Mrs. Jakelić was also charged under Article 225 (1) (2), with criminal acts against official responsibility - irrresponsible actions on duty. Namely, according to the arbitration of the District Court in Zagreb, Mrs Jakelić, during the time of her employment as the President of the Executive Council of the Center Municipality in Zagreb, signed a loan contract with the "ELAN" enterprise in the amount of 3,000,000 dinars (cca 230,000 DEM) on January 29, 1991, although she knew that "ELAN" enterprise was in a difficult financial situation, and that it is faced with bankruptcy. Since the enterprise went bankrupt soon after, this caused an immediate loss of the aforementioned amount.

Judicial consultations have discussed the possibility of annulling Article 197 of the Croatian Criminal Code concerning "the willful spread of false rumors," under which charges were brought against Mirjana Jakelić. We consider the Helsinki Watch allegations of Croatia's *curbing the freedom of expression* unjustified.

The Helsinki Watch letter claims that *the Croatian Ministry of Information has tried to close the Zagreb office of* **Borba.**

The Ministry of Information has never tried to close any newspaper office in Croatia. The conflict in the **Borba** office seems to have been a result of internal strife[13] and is presently being reviewed by a Zagreb court. Helsinki Watch fails to mention that the conflict at the **Borba** office was the result of three journalists who wanted to change the status of the office and, consequently, two were fired by **Borba's** main office in Belgrade, the capital of the country which waged war against Croatia.

Since Croatian Television is an autonomous public broadcasting company, the claim by Helsinki Watch that Croatian Television refused to air YUTEL (Yugoslav Television) for political reasons should be directed to HTV. Croatian Television was not able to broadcast YUTEL because the Croatian television broadcasting network was thoroughly destroyed in the early days of the war, and during the past cooperation with YUTEL, arose a problem of the irregular payments by YUTEL. Croatian Television was reduced from three operating channels to only one. Despite this fact, in order to ensure diversity in their coverage of events, HTV decided to air a one-hour program called "TV izbor" (TV Choice). This program presented, in integral version, different perspectives on identical news stories which were

---

[13] Cf Letter by the editor-in-chief of the **Borba** office, Seada Vranić, to the Croatian news agency HINA, November 23, 1991: "After we heard about the take-over of our office, we addressed it directly to Minister Salaj. He said that the Ministry of Information does not support the people who call themselves the Crisis Center in **Borba**, and that he is not at all involved in the described case."

In a letter answering the claims of their editor-in-chief, the Crisis Center in the Zagreb Borba office to HINA, November 24, 1991. wrote that "she (editor-in-chief, Seada Vranić), through rude insinuation, wants to drag the Croatian authorities, the Government and the Prime minister, furthermore the Ministry of Information, into our internal conflict. We state, once more, that our conflict is an internal matter and is the concern of those of us employed in the Zagreb office."

broadcast by each of the former Yugoslav republics' major television stations.[14] YUTEL stories were often covered within this program.

As a matter of principle, however, the Government of Croatia does not feel obliged, particularly not during times of war, to ensure the broadcasting of a foreign TV program, especially if it is seated in the country which waged war against Croatia.

We hope that these arguments are sufficient to assure those concerned about the freedom of the press and expression in our country that the Croatian government does everything possible, given the conditions, to affirm and strengthen these freedoms under the present conditions.[15] At the same time, we do not claim that everything is in order; on the contrary, we expect benevolent criticism and friendly help from institutions and countries which have broader experience and a better situation than our current one: post-communism and war. We are aware of the fact that we are at the beginning of a process. For the realization of a democratic society, we have both, the institutions which support one and enthusiasm.

IV. INTERFERENCE WITH THE INDEPENDENCE OF THE JUDICIARY

1. THE CASE OF DOBROSLAV PARAGA

Helsinki Watch must admit that their comments regarding the Croatian Party of Rights and its president, Dobroslav Paraga, are contradictory. On the one hand, Helsinki Watch criticizes the Croatian authorities for having brought charges against Dobroslav Paraga and on the other, for not having done it even earlier. Helsinki Watch also expresses doubts that paramilitary forces (HOS), which are incorporated into the Croatian Army are not under complete control.

The Croatian government has always made efforts not to have recourse to force and to avoid conflicts whenever possible, and also in the case when the members of the Croatian Party of Rights took possession of a building in Zagreb, as well as in the case of the integration of the soldiers which are members of the Croatian Party of Rights, into the regular

---

[14] "TV izbor" has recently been replaced with the program "Slika na sliku" (Picture on Picture), which, in a different form, presents the same variety of news perspectives previously offered by "TV izbor".

[15] - Even an extreme social critic, who won Slobodna Dalmacija Best Journalist award this year, Danko Plevnik, writes commendably on media policy, answering the question "on the role of information headquarters, decrees and other similar things": "I can freely tell you that Croatian state made lesser pressure on the media than it would seem according to some statements. In that sense our political leadership really tries to approach a developed form of democracy. However, the problem are professional convertites who simply cannot come out to an exposed position of political uncertainty, who constantly look for regime security and who openly showed their soul, a soul of regime and power...", **Slobodna Dalmacija** (Split), February 4, 1992.

Croatian armed forces. Therefore, we dismiss all the charges which are in favour of the use of force in cases when it can be avoided and the aim reached by peaceful means.

Dobroslav Paraga was acquitted of the charges and this case was closed. The trial regarding the building taken by the members of the Croatian Party of Rights is in process.

2. THE CASE OF MILE DEDAKOVIĆ

Mile Dedaković was arrested under the charges of having committed several criminal acts. The attitude of the Croatian government regarding this case, and the physical injuries inflicted upon Mile Dedaković by the Croatian Police, was presented in the Standpoints of the Government of the Republic of Croatia on Observation of Human Rights as the Response to the Letter of the U.S. Helsinki Watch Committee Dated February 13, 1992, under the Item I.

Conscription of the Judge Enver Midžić,as far as it is known to the Government, is r.ot connected with the Dedaković case. Profession is not a criterion according to which a person could be exempt from conscription. The Croatian Government will investigate the alleged threats to which, according to Helsinki Watch, Midžićhad been exposed.

V. OTHER ISSUES

1. THE ESTABLISHMENT OF THE SECRET POLICE

It should be mentioned that no irregular secret police exists in the Republic of Croatia. The National Security Service is a department of the Ministry of the Interior, while the Information Security Service is a department of the Ministry of Defense. These services, like any other legislative and executive bodies of the Republic of Croatia, must comply with the Constitution and Laws of the Republic of Croatia and function according to the legislation which regulates their existence.

2. ATTACKS ON THE JEWISH COMMUNITY CENTER AND DESECRATION OF CEMETERY

The Croatian police, as it was mentioned in the Helsinki Watch letter, has undertaken all the necessary steps and officially published invitations for a substantial reward for any fruitful information, which is not a usual practice of the Croatian police. The investigation is underway, and the Croatian police has successfully handled this case so far, although it is in the interest of the investigation that the facts are not revealed at this point. Croatian Ministry of the Interior has been in close contact with the Jewish Community, and has undertaken all measures necessary to ensure the security of the building and all personnel.

3. RESTRICTIONS ON FREEDOM OF MOVEMENT

In the war circumstances, which is understandable, restrictions on freedom of movement are necessary for numerous reasons. Among other things, due to such restrictions criminal acts decrease in number, because of being physically impeded or thwarted. This measure is directly dependent on the war conditions, and shall be abolished as soon as circumstances will allow.

4. IMPLEMENTATION OF THE CONSTITUTIONAL LAW ON HUMAN RIGHTS AND LIBERTIES AND ON RIGHTS OF THE ETHNIC AND NATIONAL COMMUNITIES OR MINORITIES IN THE REPUBLIC OF CROATIA

Implementation of the most important provisions of this law is hindered by the fact that the areas referred to in those provisions are still excluded from the Croatian legal system. However, preparations have been made on the part of the Office for National Relations to ensure the implementation of this law with an outline of measures. The project should be undertaken in cooperation with authorized departments

5. DECREASING TENSIONS BETWEEN SERBS AND CROATS

The Croatian government has lost no opportunity to normalize relations between citizens of Croatian and Serbian nationality. Nevertheless, the weight of the problem will take years to abate and to bring things back to the conditions prior to August 17th, 1990. It will be extremely difficult to revive the trust, which has taken thousands of lives of non-Serbians. Still, among the Serbs manipulated into the war against their neighbors there were also those who joined irregulars only under the threat of being killed. It is clear that those who fought on the side of the Yugoslav Army and Serbian irregulars are not automatically war criminals.

Improvement of the relations between Serbs and Croats is preconditioned by the termination of war, arrival of the United Nations peacekeeping forces and withdrawal of the Yugoslav Army and paramilitary units which came from abroad.

6. ADMINISTRATIVE DIVISION OF THE REPUBLIC OF CROATIA

The letter states that changes in the administrative division of Croatia were to diminish the number of representatives of the Serbian minority in Croatian legislative and executive bodies. On the contrary, the Croatian government supported the Draft of the Electoral Law which envisages the proportional representation of the members of the ethnic minority groups within Parliament bodies. The authors of the letter are perhaps not sufficiently acquainted with the current process of adjustment of the territorial division of the Republic of Croatia according to the provinces model, as accepted by other European states. In Croatia there are no provinces as administrative units, although they existed in the past, and this is now trying to be corrected according to the examples of such organisation in Europe. The basic territorial units, districts, remain unchanged. The administration system of provinces cannot decrease the proportional representation of Serbs in bodies of authority, because this right is guaranteed by the Constitutional Law on Human Rights and Liberties and the Rights of National and Ethnic Communities and Minorities in the Republic of Croatia, while on the parliamentary level they are put into practice by the Draft of the Electoral Law on the Elections of the Members of the Croatian Parliament, which is in the procedure of being accepted in the Parliament.[16]

---

[16] "If in the elections for the House of Representatives the representation of the elected members of ethnic and minority groups, hich is needed according to the Article 11 of this law, is not achieved, the number of the representatives in the House of Representative will be increased in order to reach the required representation, and the elected members of the parliament will be cosidered those representatives of a minority who were nominated on the state lists, but were not elected according to the proportional success of each list in the elections.

If the required representation of minority members is not reached even in the way from the former paragraph, President of the Republic of Croatia will call additional elections in as many polling districts as needed in order to achieve proportional representation. Additional elections must be called within 60 days since the first session of the new elected Parliament." (Article 27. of the Electoral Law on the Elections of the Members of the Croatian Parliament)

Letter to the Editor, The Washington Post
February 27, 1992

Serbs, Croats, and Human Rights

Helsinki Watch's report on human rights violations merits, and receives, Croatia's serious attention ["Croatia Accused of Rights Violations," news story, Feb. 15].

As in any anti-colonial war, excesses by irresponsible and uncontrolled groups do unfortunately happen.

By contrast, the excessive war crimes of which Croatians have been victims are part of a systematic *official* policy of terror. The goal has been to drive out the Croats (and other non-Serb groups) and to create an "ethnically clean," purely Serb populace in the occupied territories. Rather than banning the Serbian militia, the Yugoslav Army and Serbian authorities have armed, financed and conducted joint operations with them.

We disagree with Helsinki Watch in its assessment of our progress toward achieving our own democratic goals. Political parties are able to contest in the political arena freely. Any censorship is limited to security considerations normal for a country at war.

The unhindered access by Helsinki Watch and other such groups to Croatia is indicative of our commitment to democracy. By contrast, the occupied territories and Serbia remain off-limits to outside investigators, despite compelling evidence of extensive atrocities, the operation of concentration camps and continuing human rights violations on a massive scale.

We know that we have not yet reached a flawless society, but we have managed to lay the foundations of a new democracy, no small achievement for a country in the midst of a devasting war, a country with still over one-quarter of its territory under occupation.

BRANKO SALAJ
Minister of Information
Republic of Croatia
Zagreb

151

**APPENDIX B: HELSINKI WATCH LETTER TO
PRESIDENT FRANJO TUDJMAN REGARDING
VIOLATIONS OF FREEDOM OF EXPRESSION,
ASSOCIATION AND THE PRESS IN CROATIA,
MAY 22, 1992**

May 22, 1992

His Excellency Franjo Tudjman
President of the Republic of Croatia

Dear President Tudjman:

Helsinki Watch welcomes the positive efforts of the Croatian government to address abuses of human rights and humanitarian law in Croatia in recent months. However, Helsinki Watch is deeply disturbed by recent steps taken by the Croatian government to impede freedom of speech, expression and assembly in Croatia. In particular, we are concerned about the following cases:

. The deputy municipal prosecutor for Zagreb has requested that investigatory procedures commence against Milorad Pupovac, President of the Serbian Democratic Forum. The request was forwarded to the investigatory judge of the Zagreb district court on May 5th. According to the public prosecutor's office, Mr. Pupovac should be investigated for "spreading false information" and for "disturbing the public," because he allegedly stated that Serbian children are being forcibly converted to the Catholic religion in Croatia, a claim which the Croatian authorities deny.

Similarly, as of May 21, investigatory proceedings have been started against Globus columnist Tanja Torbarina, Danas columnist Jelena Lovric, Globus editor-in-chief Denis Kuljis and Croatian Party of Rights President, Dobroslav Paraga. The aforementioned persons reportedly have been accused of "spreading false information" and some are accused of slander. There also is some concern that similar charges will be brought against the authors of Slobodna Dalmacija's "Feral Tribune," namely Viktor Ivancic, Predrag Lucic and Boris Dezulovic.

Helsinki Watch believes that no individual should be punished for the peaceful expression of his or her views, regardless of content. Under the criminal code of the former Socialist Federal Republic of Yugoslavia, many persons -- including yourself and members of the current Croatian government -- were imprisoned for "verbal crimes." Helsinki Watch believes that Article 197 of the Croatian Criminal Code -- under which Milorad Pupovac and others are accused -- continues to criminalize speech. Helsinki Watch believes that all such laws which restrict freedom of expression, speech and the press should be repealed.

Insofar as one is accused of slander or libel, malice, reckless disregard for the truth or proof of actual temporal damages suffered by a private individual must be determined. Helsinki Watch believes that public figures and government officials cannot manipulate slander and libel laws to stifle dissent, criticism of the government or freedom of the press.

Helsinki Watch believes that the Croatian authorities have instituted investigatory proceedings against the aforementioned journalists and political figures solely because of their critical views of the Croatian government. Helsinki Watch believes that there is no basis for an investigation against any of the aforementioned individuals and calls upon the Croatian government to cease all investigatory and judicial proceedings against them.

. On May 5, 1992, a founding meeting of the Social Democratic Union was to have taken place in Zagreb. The gathering was registered with the police authorities and the meeting hall had been paid for in advance. When the delegates arrived at the meeting, they were told that the hall could not be opened for technical reasons. The organizers then contacted the local police who told them that the meeting could not take place for "security reasons." At the request of the police, the approximately 300 persons who had gathered for the meeting dispersed peacefully. Helsinki Watch is concerned that, by banning the meeting of the Social Democratic Union, the Croatian government sought to stifle the formation of an opposition party and the expression of left-of-center political views.

. In early April, the Croatian police forbid the
holding of an International Peace Conference
organized by the Croatian Anti-War Council on the
island of Vis, where Yugoslav army personnel
remain stationed. Reportedly, the meeting was
banned for "security reasons." In a letter to an
organizer of the conference, Presidential Adviser
Mario Nobilo stated that the conference could not
be held because such a meeting could be used "as
an excuse for the repression of the island's
Croatian inhabitants by Serbian forces." Mr.
Nobilo also stated that "any discussion
[regarding] the future military status of this
strategically important island can be organized
only when the Republic of Croatia regains its full
sovereignty over the island." Helsinki Watch
believes that a peaceful meeting of anti-war
activists would pose little risk of assault by
Yugoslav army forces still stationed on the
island. Moreover, the Croatian government's
restriction of discussions concerning the island's
military status is a violation of the right to
freedom of speech.

Helsinki Watch is greatly concerned that recent
steps taken by the Croatian government to restrict
freedom of assembly, speech and the press are aimed at
stifling criticism of the current government and ruling
party prior to the forthcoming elections in Croatia.
Members of the Croatian government have consistently
tried to ostracize independent journalists, political
figures and others by equating their criticism of the
Croatian government as being "traitorous to the nation"
or "supportive of Serbia's aggression against Croatia."
Helsinki Watch is concerned that such statements by
government officials have contributed to attacks
against such persons by individual extremists.

In recent days, Croatia's Public Prosecutor,
Vladimir Seks, reportedly indicated that thousands of
persons will soon be charged for "war crimes" and for
so-called "verbal crimes." Helsinki Watch urges the
Croatian government to refrain from conducting "witch
hunts" against political opponents, journalists or
others who are critical of the ruling regime or
political party.

Helsinki Watch believes that the banning of political meetings and the harassment and threat of criminal proceedings against critically-minded journalists and opposition figures is a serious impediment to the development of democracy and respect for human rights in Croatia. Helsinki Watch urges the Croatian government to respect the civil and political rights of its citizens, regardless of their political, religious, ethnic or national affiliation or orientation.

Helsinki Watch welcomes the Croatian government's past response to the concerns of the international human rights community. We trust that you will give careful consideration to our recent concerns and take steps to protect the civil and political rights of Croatia's citizens.

Respectfully,

Jeri Laber
Executive Director

APPENDIX C: Human Rights Watch/Helsinki Policy Statement on Citizenship Legislation in the Republics of the Former Socialist Federal Republic of Yugoslavia (SFRJ)

This policy statement addresses the effects of new citizenship laws on the rights of only those individuals who resided in a republic of the the the former SFRJ at the time of each republic's independence, and not the rights of new immigrants (i.e., people who applied for citizenship after the republic's declarations of independence or after the dissolution of the SFRJ).

We believe that principles of international human rights must be used to evaluate the proposed citizenship laws. This policy statement identifies some of the considerations that we urge all ex-republics to take into account in fashioning their laws.

A. General Considerations

1. Applicability of International Human Rights Law in All Republics Formerly Part of the SFRJ

The requirements of customary international human rights law are fully in force with the effect of law in the republics of the former SFRJ. In addition, the SFRJ had ratified and accepted many of the major human rights treaties and other international documents. Croatia, Bosnia-Hercegovina, Slovenia and Macedonia have either expressly acceded to most international human rights documents or have acknowledged their applicability. The same states also have formally accepted the OSCE human rights agreements.

On April 27, 1992, the former SFRJ republics of Serbia and Montenegro joined to form a rump Yugoslav state, the Federal Republic of Yugoslavia (FRY), but it remains largely unrecognized by the international community. Nevertheless, the FRY has expressed its wish to be recognized as the successor state to the SFRJ and thereby retain membership in international organizations. Such a statement also implies that the FRY is willing to accede to international agreements to which the former SFRJ was a party. Therefore, for the purposes of this policy statement, all international obligations assumed by the former SFRJ will be transferred to the FRY.

2. The Need to Strengthen Rather Than Diminish Protection of Human Rights in the Republics of the Former SFRJ

It is a moral, political, and legal obligation of each of the republics of the former SFRJ to protect human rights within its territory. In no event should the establishment of independence serve as a pretext for cutting back on the rights to which former citizens of the former SFRJ are entitled under international human rights law.

3. The Obligation to Ensure Protection of the Rights of All Persons Subject to Governmental Authority, Whether or Not They Are Formally "Citizens"

Most aspects of international human rights law apply to "everyone" or to "all persons," regardless of citizenship or nationality. A government's obligations do not end with ensuring the rights of only its citizens.

4. The Obligation to Minimize Statelessness

Because citizenship is the principal mechanism through which people take part in governmental affairs, it is incumbent on the former republics to develop and implement their citizenship laws in a manner that avoids rendering individuals stateless. We therefore urge the new states of the former SFRJ to ratify the 1961 Convention Relating to the Status of Stateless Persons.[218]

5. Obligations With Respect to Persons Who May Also Have Links to Another State or Republic

Avoidance of statelessness does not exhaust the responsibilities of the new states with respect to persons who may have links to more than one republic or state. If proposed citizenship legislation would adversely affect an individual's human rights, objection on human rights grounds is warranted even if he or she qualifies for citizenship (or another status such as permanent residence or asylum) in another state.

---

[218] Croatia is a party to the Convention.

6. Prohibition of Arbitrary Deprivation of Citizenship

Under Article 15 of the International Covenant, a person may not be arbitrarily deprived of citizenship (nationality).

B. Specific Considerations

1. Claims Based on Duration of Residence and Reasonable Expectations

In the context of the dissolution of the SFRJ, claims based on a reasonable expectation of continuing residence deserve special attention. Disrupting expected residence may impose serious hardships on individuals whose jobs, families, and other relationships depend upon being able to continue living where they have been living. International human rights principles safeguard the reasonable expectations of individuals who, as citizens of the former SRFJ, have been living in one of the former republics that has now established independence. The rights of those individuals to continue in their habitual residence should not be impaired because of political changes in the world around them.

Two sets of citizenship requirements would therefore be preferable: one applicable to people who settled in the former republic before the establishment of independence and one applicable to those migrating to it thereafter. This arrangement prevents imposing a hardship on those residents who could not have reasonably foreseen a change in their legal status.

Persons with established ties of residence to a former republic should be presumptively eligible for citizenship in the state the republic has become, whether or not other criteria for citizenship (such as *jus soli* or *jus sanguinis*[219]) would be

---

[219] Under the principle of *jus soli*, one gains citizenship by dint of being born on the territory of a country. U.S. citizenship is based on the principle of *jus soli*. The child of a non-citizen born in the U.S. automatically becomes a citizen.

Jus sanguinis is the principle by which one acquires citizenship through, literally, "blood." One is considered a citizen of country X if his or her parents were also citizens of country X. The German, and many European, systems of granting citizenship are based on the principle of *jus sanguinis*. For example, a child of Turkish migrant workers born in Berlin does not automatically acquire German citizenship. However, an ethnic German born

met. Accordingly, Human Rights Watch/Helsinki opposes any proposed citizenship laws that mandate excessively long periods of residence or other restrictive conditions as a qualification for citizenship for persons who were citizens of the SFRJ with a settled place of residence in the former republic at the time of independence.

Persons with a reasonable expectation of continued residence who do not elect or qualify for citizenship of that state should be allowed to remain in their place of habitual residence in any event, and to return there after temporary absences. Human Rights Watch/Helsinki opposes any bills or laws that require involuntary change of residence, whether or not the affected persons are "citizens."

2. Claims Based on Family Ties

International human rights law, e.g. Article 23 of the International Covenant on Civil and Political Rights, protects the family as a social unit and the right of persons to marry and found a family. Proposals that give greater weight to an individual's ancestry or ethnicity than to his or her present circumstances could disrupt family life by allocating citizenship entitlement to one but not both spouses, to a child and one parent but not to the other parent, or on other similarly arbitrary lines. For the reasons previously suggested, political changes extraneous to an existing family unit should not impair the rights or expectations of the members of that unit. Accordingly, Human Rights Watch/Helsinki opposes citizenship proposals that would have the effect of arbitrarily dividing a family into citizens and non-citizens.

3. Proposed Disqualifications on Grounds Such as Medical Needs, Criminal Status or Political Affiliation

Certain citizenship proposals deny eligibility for citizenship in a country to persons who have been convicted of a crime or who were under criminal prosecution, have received treatment for alcoholism or drug addiction, or who belong or have belonged to certain political groups such as the Communist Party apparatus.

a. Denying citizenship to previously convicted criminals effectively adds an additional, *ex post facto*, and heavier penalty to the convicted person's

---

in Russia is automatically considered a German citizen even if his or her ancestors left Germany two hundred years earlier.

punishment. Imposing penalties heavier than those that applied at the time a crime was committed violates Article 15 of the ICCPR.

b. Excluding persons who have received treatment for alcoholism or drug addiction is a cruel punishment that would discourage people from seeking needed treatment. Article 7 of the ICCPR, which prohibits "inhumane or degrading treatment or punishment," protects individuals against this exclusion. Denying citizenship on these grounds creates a new penalty that represents an attempt to criminalize an individual's past act of having registered at a clinic for substance abuse. Finally, it creates categories of people who are targets of discrimination on the basis of status or state of being that is beyond their control. This kind of discrimination is forbidden by Article 26 of the ICCPR.

c. Excluding categorically persons who worked for the Yugoslav Army (JNA), the League of Communists or any other institution, on the grounds that they perpetrated grave abuses of human rights, collectively punishes individuals and violates the ICCPR's Article 22 (on freedom of association). Before such a person is denied citizenship, he or she should be *individually* proven culpable in a court of law for specific crimes that were outlawed at the time of the acts in question. The record of each citizenship applicant should be judged individually, with the appropriate recourse to judicial institutions.

Even though similar political and medical tests are or have been used as criteria for immigration or naturalization eligibility in various countries (including the United States), Human Rights Watch/Helsinki believes that a fundamentally different situation is presented when such criteria are applied not to determine eligibility for admission of new entrants into a given state, but rather to determine how citizenship entitlements should be allocated when an existing state (such as the SFRJ) fragments into smaller units. Persons falling into the above medical, political, or similar categories were already citizens of the SFRJ; by virtue of falling into these categories, they could not have been involuntarily expatriated by the SFRJ. They should not be worse off by virtue of political developments occurring in the territory of the former SFRJ.

Human Rights Watch/Helsinki opposes eligibility tests such as those suggested above, to the extent that they are applied to deny citizenship to persons whose ties with the former republics would otherwise qualify them for citizenship.[220]

---

[220] Because different equitable considerations are at issue, this policy statement does not address whether any of the above criteria would be legitimate if applied to admission of new entrants (i.e., to immigrants, or to naturalization of persons who would not otherwise qualify for citizenship).

APPENDIX D: The Croatian Interior Ministry's Overview of the Commission of Crimes in Croatia From 1991 to July 1, 1993, Including Those Perpetrated by Members of the Croatian Police[221]

Republic of Croatia
Ministry of Internal Affairs
Criminal Police Division

Zagreb, August 13, 1993

SURVEY OF MURDERS AND OTHER CRIMINAL OFFENSES
COMMITTED BY MEMBERS OF THE POLICE FORCE BETWEEN 1991
AND JULY 1, 1993

In the territory of the Republic of Croatia, more specifically in that part of the territory which is under the authority of government institutions of the Republic of Croatia, the following murders and attempted murders have been registered:

- during 1991: 714 murders, of which 203 cases remain unsolved (rate of cases solved 71.3 percent),

- during 1992: 668 murders, of which 162 cases remain unsolved (rate of cases solved 75.7 percent),

- between January 1 and May 31, 1993: 121 murders, of which twenty-four cases remain unsolved (rate of cases solved 80.25 percent).

Of the above-listed number of murders between 1992 and July 1, 1993, the criminal offense of murder was committed by thirty-four members of the police force, while the criminal offense of attempted murder was committed by ten

---

[221] The document that follows was translated by a Human Rights Watch/Helsinki researcher. Copies of the original text and appendices to the text are available from Human Rights Watch/Helsinki.

members. The criminal offense of rape was committed by one member of the police force, while the criminal offense of attempted rape was committed by one member of the police force.

The abuse of civilians was reflected in the form of the following criminal offenses: the criminal offense of inflicting serious bodily harm was committed by thirty-five members of the police force; the criminal offense of violent behavior was committed by eight members; the criminal offense of robbery was committed by twelve members; and the criminal offense of illegal seizure of publicly-owned immovable property was committed by fourteen members of the police force.

Regarding the criminal offense of murder in its most aggravated form as described in the Criminal Code of the Republic of Croatia, we list in chronological order the most characteristic instances that occurred in the territory of the Republic of Croatia, in which cases the perpetrators were members of the police force:

- On September 21, 1991, on the Koranski bridge in Karlovac, policeman Mihajlo Hrastov from the Karlovac Police District committed several murders against Jovan Sitić and twelve other persons and the criminal offense of attempted murder. Criminal charges were filed against Mihajlo Hrastov with Karlovac's District Public Prosecutor on September 22, 1991, under number 511-05-12/3-4-K-640/91.

- On August 26, 1991, the murder of Ilija Martić was committed in the "Viktorija" restaurant in Sisak. On August 27, 1991, based on a well-founded suspicion that he had committed the criminal offense of murder, Salid Masinović, a member of the reserve police force in the Sisak police district, was arrested and criminal charges were filed against him under number 511-10-02-K-588/91 and he was brought before an investigative judge of the Sisak district court on August 27, 1991.

- On November 15, 1991, along with a special report filed under number 511-08-52-K-362/91, the following members of the Pula police district were brought before the investigative judge of the Pula district court: Zdenko Tomajić, Niko Barun, Mario Juzvišen, Ivan Strmecki and Marijan Skvor, based on a well-founded suspicion that they had committed the criminal offense of murder against Srbislav Petrov from Umag.

- On January 19, 1992, in the town of Brez, in the municipality of Sisak, Ivan Preml, a member of the police force shot and killed Ivica Bobinc [sic], also a member of the police force, with a machine-gun.

- On January 9, 1992, in Pakrac, Darko Musulin, a member of the police force, killed policeman Zdravko Pemper.

- On March 17, 1992, in the Daruvar police station, members of the police force (i.e., Željko Kurin, Ivica Molnar and Franjo Kalem) murdered Lazo Slavuljević, a civilian.

- In Blinski Kut, in the municipality of Sisak, members of the police force (i.e., Stanislav Gavron and Ivan Hubelić) murdered a civilian with the use of firearms.

- On June 20, 1992, in Rijeka, Tomislav Gujić, a member of the police force, killed Milovan Lovričić, a civilian, with a revolver.

- On July 18, 1992, in Ivanić Grad, Mladen Horvat, a member of the police force, committed the murder of Zlatko Sprajacek with a revolver.

- On July 22, 1992, in Zagreb, Zlatko Segina, a member of the police force, killed Snježana Pernar, a civilian, with a revolver.

- On August 22, 1992, in the Crikvenica police station building, a member of the police force, Ljuban Cavrak, killed Vanja Maričić, a civilian, with a revolver.

- On October 12, 1992, in Vambladon, in the municipality of Pula, Dražen Kordiš, a member of the police force, killed Ljubomir Boromiš, also a member of the police force, with a revolver.

- On October 22, 1992, in Kašteli, a member of the police force, Ante Bilandžić, killed Dejan Božanić, a member of the HV (Croatian Army), with a revolver.

- On November 9, 1992, in Sisak, Luka Susec, a member of the police force, killed Ivo Perkov, a civilian.

- On November 26, 1992, in Podravska Slatina, members of the police force (i.e., Dragan Petković, Goran Draksler, Filip Dorčak and Zvonko Zrišnjak) murdered Djuro Kolundžija.

- On December 3, 1992, in Makarska, Goran Baković, a member of the police force, murdered of another member of the police force, Marko Kaliger.

- On December 22, 1992, in Senj, Petar Klobučar, a member of the police force, murdered Vesna Bjondić, a civilian.

- On August 8, 1992, Željko Polanec, a member of the border police station at Čakovec, murdered Seval Bajrić and Damir Poja.

- On September 21, 1991, members of the Zagreb Police District force (i.e., Željko Vučemilović-Grgić, Branko Matošević, Željko Ceko, and Paško Palić) murdered Ante Paradžik and committed the criminal offense of attempted murder against Branko Perković.

- On August 17, 1991, in Zagreb, M. Pavić, a member of the Zagreb police district force, murdered Miroslav Mikulić.

- On February 19, 1992, Dinko Mijatović, a member of the Slatina police station, committed the murder of Nikola Kosić.

- On March 19, 1993, in Senj, Damir Sertić, a member of the Pula district police force, murdered Miroslav Prodanić.

- On May 1, 1991, members of the Pakrac police station (i.e., Ivan Blažinović and Željko Vozić) attempted to kill Ivan Bencek with a revolver.

- On July 18, 1992, in Beslincuo, in the municipality of Ivanić Grad, Mladen Horvat, a member of the Kutina district police, murdered Zlatko Spajceg.

In all the above-listed cases and in other instances not specifically described as characteristic cases here, criminal charges were filed with the competent government authorities after criminal procedures were conducted. Also, members of the police force - listed in the Survey of Criminal Offenses Committed According to Qualification and Number, Committed by Members of the Police Force Between 1991 and July 1, 1993 - were subjected to criminal procedures, criminal charges were filed against them with the competent government authorities and disciplinary proceedings were enacted, which were cited as bases for their discharge from the Ministry of Internal Affairs.

From the beginning of the armed rebellion in the territory of the Republic of Croatia the following have been registered:

- in 1990: seventy-two explosions and one fire;

- in 1991: 1,881 explosions and 258 fires, in which 1,257 objects belonging to citizens of Serbian nationality were damaged;

- in 1992: 3,302 explosions and 1,025 fires, in which 3,158 objects belonging to citizens of Serbian nationality were damaged;

- in January 1993: ninety-two explosions and thirty-four fires, in which seventy-eight objects belonging to citizens of Serbian nationality were damaged;

- in February 1993: 104 explosions and forty-nine fires, in which ninety-three objects belonging to citizens of Serbian nationality were damaged;

- in March 1993: eighty-three explosions and forty-six fires, in which forty-nine objects belonging to citizens of Serbian nationality were damaged;

- in April 1993: eighty-three explosions and thirty-six fires, in which forty-four objects belonging to citizens of Serbian nationality were damaged;

- in May 1993: sixty-seven explosions and twenty-five fires, in which forty-oneobjects belonging to citizens of Serbian nationality were damaged;

- in June 1993: fifty explosions and thirteen fires, in which twenty-five objects belonging to citizens of Serbian nationality were damaged.

In all the above-listed cases, criminal charges have been filed with the competent government authorities after operative-criminal and criminal-technical procedures were conducted. As a result of the aggression on the Republic of Croatia, it was not feasible to exercise control over the entire internationally-recognized territory of the Republic of Croatia. The general state of war that existed in the territory of the Republic of Croatia helped the perpetrators of criminal offenses and prevented the police from discovering the majority of the perpetrators of these criminal offenses.

Up to this point we possess information regarding 227 perpetrators against whom operative and criminal procedures have been conducted, against whom criminal charges have been filed and who have been handed over to the competent prosecuting authorities. During criminal proceedings, it has been determined that sixty-nine of the [227] perpetrators were members of the police force against whom criminal charges were filed for the commission of the criminal offense of endangering life and property by means of a generally dangerous action or tool, while criminal charges for the commission of the criminal offense of terrorism were filed against four members of the police force.

The efficiency of solving these criminal offenses is reflected in the rate of cases solved which was:

- in 1991: 16.2 percent;

- in 1992: 17.6 percent;

- in the first six months of 1993: 15 percent.

Annexed to this report are:

1. tables depicting arson fires in the territories of police districts[222]
2. a survey of criminal offenses committed.

Chief of the Division
Ivan Gatarić

---

[222] These graphs are not included here but can be obtained from Human Rights Watch/Helsinki.

SURVEY
of criminal offenses, according to qualification and number of perpetrators,
committed by members of the police force between 1991 and July 1, 1993

Article 35. KZ RH[223]	MURDER 34
Article 35/19 KZ RH	ATTEMPTED MURDER 10
Article 38. KZ RH	MANSLAUGHTER 7
Article 41. KZ RH	SERIOUS BODILY INJURY 35
Article 43. KZ RH	PARTICIPATION IN A FIGHT 12
Article 51. KZ RH	ENDANGERING SAFETY 2
Article 83. KZ RH	RAPE 1
Article 83/19. KZ RH	ATTEMPTED RAPE 1
Article 130. KZ RH	LARCENY 21
Article 131. KZ RH	GRAND LARCENY 66
Article 132. KZ RH	ROBBERY 12
Article 140. KZ RH	ILLEGAL SEIZURE OF PUBLICLY-OWNED IMMOVABLE PROPERTY . . 14
Article 142. KZ RH	FRAUD 17
Article 153. KZ RH	ENDANGERING LIFE OR PROPERTY BY MEANS OF A GENERALLY DANGEROUS ACTION OR TOOL . . . 69

---

[223] i.e., Criminal Code of the Republic of Croatia (Krivični Zakon (KZ) Republike Hrvatske (RH))